It's Been a *Long Trip, but a Lot of Fun*

FRAN WICKES

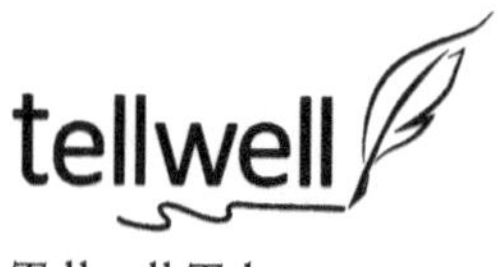

Tellwell Talent
www.tellwell.ca

ISBN
978-0-2288-6358-8 (Hardcover)
978-0-2288-6357-1 (Paperback)
978-0-2288-6359-5 (eBook)

DESCRIPTION

VILLAGE LIFE IN THE 1940S IN ENGLAND, followed by family tragedy. This led to unusual moves during my early years, a career choice that gave me access to the world. Emigration to Australia opened a whole new world that I felt had to be explored.

Beginning in Hobart in Tasmania I spent the next six years crisscrossing the whole country working as a midwife in both city and country locations.

Then I travelled over to New Zealand and with a friend we worked as waitresses in both North and South islands. In our off-duty times, we visited many of the well-known tourist destinations, but when winter arrived, we both craved warmth and sunshine so returned to Australia.

Back to Perth and more training, a brief marriage for me before I headed back to Darwin. At this stage of my life, I needed a challenge, and I knew that there were plenty of opportunities in the Territory. After I retired, my interest in craft revived and I developed a craft industry, selling my creations worldwide, plus being a marketeer for 18 years. Now in my eightieth decade I am still exploring from a quite different angle. It has been a long trip, but it has never been dull.

Table of Contents

AN UNFORTUNATE BEGINNING

AN OLD, BATTERED BABY'S PRAM is parked under a branch of a weeping willow tree, with the grassy bank sloping down toward the river. There are the sounds of birds and water falling over a weir in the distance.

It's a balmy, sunny afternoon. The baby in the pram gazes up at the play of light and shadow through the leaves. The pram rocks momentarily, then begins to roll slowly over the grass toward the river. A dog barks loudly to alert the family. Shouts of alarm and the sound of footsteps. The pram stops with a jerk.

This is my only memory of life at the old mill where I was born in the village of Ab Kettleby. It was the spring of 1938, and I was the four-month-old baby in the pram. I didn't receive an explanation until many years later.

It seems that one of my sisters was not happy with all the attention being bestowed on the new baby, so she quietly released the pram brake and watched as it rolled toward the weir. Fortunately, the dog raised the alarm and one of the farm workers arrested the runaway pram just before it fell into the river.

My mother was pregnant with my oldest sister when she and my father married. Both were in their early thirties at that time. The next child was born six years later, and I was born two years after that. I was a disappointment as they had hoped for a boy; third time lucky.

I have no idea when the family moved into Melton Mowbray, the nearest town, as I have no memories of our new home apart from when we three children were put to bed in the downstairs front room. This must have been during the war, when it would have been difficult to move three children down the rather steep staircase in the house in a hurry in the night if there was a bombing raid.

Our mother died suddenly during the night when I was three years old. Although I tried over the years to find out more of the circumstances of that fateful night, no one would tell me anything. Her death was listed as 'cardiac asthma' on the death certificate. My entire world disappeared overnight.

It was the custom at the time to bless children with two sets of godparents. One pair would usually be an older couple. They would have experience of the world and be able to offer advice to the growing child as needed.

The other pair should be younger and able to provide up-to-date assistance. Putting up your hand up to be a godparent was not just a matter of looking good and not dropping the baby at the christening; you had to be prepared to lend a more practical hand.

I have no recollection of that night but no doubt my father was shattered by the turn of events and did the best he knew how at the time. There were very few telephones in those days, so either he or one of the neighbours went to give news of her death to her brother, who lived with his wife and family in the centre of town.

They already had two children, but they took we three in until others could be notified and asked for help. I have no idea why he handed his children over, but as he was a shift worker at a nearby steelworks, it would have been difficult to care for us himself.

My eldest sister stayed with that family until she was old enough to leave home, and my middle sister was placed with her young godparents who had one child already. I went to live with my older godparents, probably because they were easier to contact.

I had never met them and only ever knew them as Mr and Mrs Ringrose. I have no memory of our first meeting, but it was not long before I took to screaming loud and long whenever Mr Ringrose came anywhere near me.

He was rather fond of fondling little girls, and this little girl did not appreciate such behaviour.

Eventually, Mrs Ringrose took me to visit my older sister and mentioned my screaming fits to Aunt Mary. This rang alarm bells in her head, so she took me outside to her garden.

She must have asked the right questions because she then took me up to her bedroom, to be shown something. She found that I had bruises and marks where no three-year-old should have such things, so she raised the alarm and I stayed with her until other arrangements could be made.

Many years later, Aunt Mary told me that Mrs Ringrose discovered her husband had also molested their two daughters. He was their father, so they assumed it was normal. It was only as they reached their teens that they realised that kind of behaviour was not the norm.

I met my younger godparents on the railway station platform. I had never seen them before either and was trying to size them up when the train arrived.

This was the first time I had seen a steam engine— very large, very loud, and hissing steam at all angles. From my perspective on the platform there was also a large dark space between the train and the platform. This was all very scary, and I began to cry. In response I received a sharp tap across the back of my legs from my godmother.

'Nice little girls don't cry, so stop that noise,' she said.

I have no recollection of that train journey, but that response from my godmother set the tone for our relationship. It never really improved. With hindsight, I can understand her reaction.

Connie, my father's youngest sister, was the youngest in a family of nine children, so she had no actual experience with young children such as me. She and Bob had been married for three years, and there were no signs of children of their own, so apparently my father gave me to them as a ready-made family. Much later in life I discovered that Bob had contracted mumps at a critical time in his life, so he was probably sterile anyway.

EASTON ON THE HILL

Bob had lived in the village all his life, so when he married Connie and brought her to the village, she was an 'outsider' and didn't have any childhood friends in the area.

There was only one other small child at the end of the village where we lived. Her mother had been a schoolteacher, so she considered herself socially a step above Connie.

Although I began to play with Margaret, who was a year younger than me, her mother was always referred to as Mrs H; she and Connie were never on first-name terms.

Bob sang tenor in the church choir, so Connie took me to church when she sometimes attended evensong with him. Someone suggested to her that she should join the Mothers' Union to find a friend and gather tips on raising a small child. This idea came to nothing, as the chairperson deemed Connie didn't qualify as she had not actually carried me in her womb.

There was a definite hierarchy within the village, much of it related to the occupation of the man of the house. The wives of the leading men took charge of the social order within such things as the Mothers' Union, the Women's Institute and organising whist drives and the bridge club.

The pecking order began with the rector's sister. He was unmarried, and his sister kept house for him. Then there was the lady who lived in the Hall, a very large imposing house. I've no idea what her husband did, but he was top of the pile as it were. She was a rather tall, very erect lady, and she and her husband occupied one of the front pews in the church that had a little box around it.

There was the wife of a solicitor, then the wife of a dentist, followed by the various farmers' wives. None of the farmers owned any of their land, it was all leased out as part of the Burghley estate, and the largest holding was top of the pile.

It seems strange by today's standards when people are used to introducing each other by their Christian names and sometimes it might be years before you realise whether a couple are married or not, but at that time social standing and having a marriage licence was very important.

Bob had a mate called Dennis Drudge. They had gone to school together, but both Bob and Connie only ever referred to his wife as Mrs Drudge, never anything more personal, as she was the daughter of a judge.

We lived in Jasmine Cottage, which was on the street leading to the church. It had jasmine growing on a trellis over the door. There was one basic room downstairs with the staircase enclosed to the right of the door.

This enclosure went to the back wall so that the space under the stairs was hidden from view. There was an extra bit built onto the back wall of the cottage as well. This had a window that gave light to the area.

This was the scullery with the far end being the pantry. There was one actual bedroom upstairs, so a large landing was made into my bedroom. It was large enough for a single bed, a small bedside cabinet, and a large chest of drawers.

Like all the houses in the village at that time, there was no running water at all on the property. A wealthy benefactor of the village in years past had paid for water from a spring to be piped into the village, with taps placed in each street.

Water was collected in buckets from these taps. Just about every house had a rainwater tank somewhere on the property, and we always used rainwater for tea. After the first frost of the winter, the pipes to the street taps had to be lagged to prevent them from freezing and possibly bursting later.

Outside on the other side of a small lawn area was the washhouse. The far end of this was the toilet, a well-polished wooden top with the bucket placed strategically under the hole, and squares of torn up newspaper. Toilet rolls were not to be had until after the war.

There was the copper for boiling the water for doing laundry and heating the water for the weekly bath. The end nearest to the house was where they stored the coal.

Monday, of course, was wash day for clothes and bedding with a small mangle being brought out from the washhouse onto the path.

Clothes were popped into the copper to wash in the hot water with grated washing soap flakes, then Connie lifted them out and put them through the mangle before tossing them into a tin wash tub with some Reckitts Blue in it to be rinsed.

Then Connie mangled them again and hung them on the line which stretched across the little garden area to the house. This meant that the washing was on display to all and sundry as they went up and down the street, hence a strict protocol dictated that underwear or tatty items were always hung nearest the house!

Village life in the 1940s was simpler, I suppose, but harder too. No modern appliances and no frills. In what I considered to be my village, each house had their own outside toilet, and the 'dunny man' came round on Tuesdays to take used buckets to his cart and replace it with another one.

Consequently, if you were in the habit of inviting friends round for lunch, you never had a lunch party on Tuesday; sometimes the 'pong' took a while to disperse.

There were also regular visitors to the villages. The man from the co-op called to take orders that would be delivered during the week. My aunt took advantage of this to order the heavy items like flour, sugar and cooking salt which came in a large block that had to be grated for use.

Then the man from the Prudential came round to collect instalments on life assurance policies and such. Various other tradesmen drove small vans round the villages, too, selling fish, meat, and bread. Add to them the delivery of coal, chopped wood and less often the rag and bone man. I used to wonder what kind of bones he collected but never got what I thought of as a straight answer.

Uncle Bob had gone to work at a timber yard in the town when he left school, and he worked for the same firm for the rest of his life, moving up the ladder as he became more skilled.

It was during his apprenticeship that he managed to lop the top off one thumb and part of a finger on the other hand, thus rendering him as unsuitable for call up to the army.

He rode a motorcycle to work each day with a knapsack on his back containing his snacks, lunch, and a thermos of tea. When he returned home in the evening, his knapsack contained two lumps of firewood. These were then added to the stack tucked in the far corner of the yard. When I was old enough, I was taught how to split some of these logs into kindling for the fire. This became one of my Saturday morning chores for many years.

Friday evening was bath time. The tin bath would be placed in front of the fire, hot water from the copper brought in and added to the cold water already placed in the bath.

Then it was my turn to be bathed and dried off, given supper, and taken up to bed. Connie and Bob had their turns before they went to bed. Hair washing was done in the bath with rinsing water being poured over the head into the bath. Hair would be towelled as dry as possible, then we knelt on the hearth rug in front of the fire to get it dry.

When I was a bit older, I remember scanning the rag rug to find bits of old clothes that I recognised while I dried my hair.

All clothes that couldn't be patched yet again were given to my grandmother to cut up and weave into rag rugs. When we eventually moved from soap to shampoo after the war, Friday was known as Amami night, that being the name of the first shampoo on the shelves.

Friday night was also when I received a dose of syrup of figs, a palatable laxative. Connie believed in a 'good clear-out' at least once a week!

Connie had left school at the age of fourteen and gone to work at a local 'big house.' She began her life there as a scullery maid, washing up pots and cleaning vegetables.

As other staff left (usually to get married), she moved up the ladder and ended her working days there as the under cook. She deputised for the cook when she had a day off, so she certainly knew how to cook well. When she married Bob, her employment was automatically terminated because she now had the responsibility of making a home for her husband while producing a family.

At one stage during the war, the meat ration was four ounces per person per week. Offal was never included in the ration, so if the butcher had killed during the week, he might have heart, kidneys, or liver for sale, plus rabbits and sometimes hares too.

Connie knew how to make a meal from any of those, so we lived quite well. Demonstrations of affection from Connie were very limited; food was her love offering, and if I ate what was on my plate that was enough for her.

I took a dislike to bread-and-butter pudding for some reason or other when I was about five years old. Connie gave me a small serving when I went home from school for lunch, but I turned up my nose and refused to eat it.

She told me I would have to eat it at teatime. While she and Bob ate meat and vegetables, I was presented with the bread-and-butter pudding, nothing else! I still refused to eat it and went to bed hungry.

Bob remonstrated with her, but she was determined that no child was going to defy her! At breakfast time, said pudding was brought out yet again, so I went to school where one of the teachers gave me some biscuits. When I came home for lunch, Connie came to the table carrying the hated pudding, but she tripped and broke the rim of the dish. She felt she could not offer me a plate of food that might have broken china in it. I understand that bread and butter pudding is delicious, but I have never eaten it since that day.

Over the years I have pondered long and hard about my non-relationship with Connie. She and Bob provided me with the necessities of life—food, shelter, and education—and I guess she loved me in her own way, but it would have been so much better with a few hugs and kisses thrown in.

I always felt that Bob would have liked to be more demonstrative, but in view of my experiences with Mr Ringrose all those years before he was wary of any such moves being misinterpreted.

Bob inherited his childhood home when his father died two days after his mother's funeral. I have no idea why he got the house as he had two brothers. One lived in the village and the other in the town of Stamford. Their only sister had married an American and lived in Boston in the USA.

The inherited house was in a state of disrepair, but there was a large garden attached. Connie and Bob spent all their leisure time growing fruit, vegetables, and a variety of flowers.

Apart from the garden beds, there were several apple trees, a plum tree, several black currant bushes, white and red currant bushes, and gooseberry bushes, too, so there was plenty of scope for jams, jellies, and bottled fruit for winter use.

Living with Bob and Connie was very different from living with my parents and two sisters, and I had to find out what the rules and limits were in this new place. In the evenings after the cooked tea was cleared away, Bob and Connie liked to sit and read, so I consider myself very fortunate that they taught me to read at a very early age and supplied me with a few children's books.

No reading matter was off limits, and if I found a word, I didn't understand I knew where they kept the dictionary and was encouraged to look for the word. I'm sure others are aware of the trap that dictionaries pose; you start looking for one word and end up perusing the whole page, but it's still fun.

The wireless was only turned on for a few select programs and the national news. The sounds of Big Ben chiming meant I had to be quiet because it was time for the news or a government announcement.

Connie listened to *Mrs Dale's Diary* most afternoons, and they were both fans of the program *It's That Man Again* (ITMA). One evening each week after I had gone to bed they would listen to a serial program called *Appointment with Fear*. 'The Royal Scotsman Theme' opened the show and it was introduced by Valentine Dyall, who had a very deep voice.

It quite often ended in screams or the sound of a gun firing, then the theme music again. There was often silence for a long time at the end, and I would lie in bed wondering if the noise had been on the wireless or if it was real.

Sometimes when Connie wanted to go shopping, get her hair cut on her own, or if she was finding me difficult to manage, she would leave me with 'courtesy aunts.'

Aunt Nellie was my favourite. I don't know how Connie became acquainted with her, but I really enjoyed spending time there.

She was not bound by tradition. If I was there on a Monday and it was raining, she would put off doing the washing and think of something else to do that I could help her with. She taught me to play ludo and we did jigsaws together.

Later she also gave me my very first birthday party. Something about birthdays came into our conversation, and I told her I didn't have those.

I explained that because I was almost a Christmas baby, I always had to wait 'til Christmas to get my birthday presents and everyone was too busy to think of birthday parties. Aunt Nellie thought about that for a moment and said that if the King could have a special birthday when it wasn't really one, so could I!

She gave me a birthday party in July, and she baked a cake and put six and a half candles on it. You know how precious those halves were at that age.

I had quite a few 'courtesy aunts' over the years, and I have happy memories of my times with all of them. This meant that sometimes I went to other village schools, but my ability to read meant it didn't seem to affect my progress through the system.

I was allowed to play with Margaret, the girl who lived opposite us in the village. We have kept in touch over all the years, and I just wish we lived a bit closer now that we are both old ladies.

Margaret's house had quite a large garden and yard. It made a wonderful play space for us—a plank over a log made a marvellous seesaw, and there was lots of stuff to make little houses with.

I was sometimes allowed to go over there during evenings in the winter. They had a nice sitting room with a nice fireplace and carpet on the floor. Her mother also had some old clothes that she allowed us to play with for 'dress-ups.'

Her parents usually had the wireless tuned to pleasant music, and we were allowed to go into the front hall to dance in our dressy clothes. The program was by the Palm Court Orchestra who played waltzes and polkas, lovely swishing music.

One evening Mr H came home while we were dancing, and Mrs H came down their staircase as he entered. Without hesitation he began dancing with his wife, and he kissed her at the end of the dance.

When I returned home from these little outings Connie would ask after Mr and Mrs H, and this evening I mentioned that they had danced together and kissed! It was such an unusual event that never happened in our house. Even though Connie and Bob had only been married three years, there was never any overt expression of love or affection between them. I never saw them hold hands, kiss, or hold each other in a loving way.

VILLAGE SOCIAL LIFE

In those days most of the married women stayed at home doing all the daily chores without the aid of all the modern inventions; no take-away meals or packet mixes, and the village didn't even have a fish and chip shop. There were very few motor cars, so you either walked, rode a bicycle, or caught the infrequent bus service that ran between Kettering and Stamford and called at the villages on the way.

The Church Army Hut was the only place for social gatherings. The members of the Women's Institute had their meetings there, and it was also the location for wedding receptions, occasional dances, and children's parties.

It had a very good sprung wooden floor which was excellent for dancing, but it had to be polished for such events. I can't remember how I came to be included, but I do remember being there for one of the polishing sessions. Candle grease was melted and blobs of it thrown from the tin onto the floor fairly widely spaced, then any child or able-bodied person tied old rags to their feet, and we slipped all over the place, spreading the grease and giving the floor a high polish.

Children's parties were usually to celebrate some event or other. Trestle tables would be put out with benches for us to sit on. During winter we had to take our slippers and change into them when we arrived, so we didn't track mud all over the floor. We carried a bag with our cup, saucer, plate, and spoon so the ladies providing the food did not have a pile of washing up to do, apart from the fact that the Hut may not have had much equipment either. There would be jam sandwiches, probably some fish paste ones, small rock cakes (which lived up to their name) and jelly and custard.

I also remember weak cordial to drink. After tea, the trestles would be removed, and some chairs brought out for a game of musical chairs with someone playing music on the old piano. Sometimes the adults organised three-legged races the length of the hall and various other ploys for us to express our excitement, and the party usually finished with us all being assembled for a giant conga line.

Mrs Perkins, one of the senior school mistresses, seemed to be the one who organised bus outings for the village. In springtime there was usually at least one outing to tour the tulip fields in the Spalding area.

Such tours were of no particular interest to children, but children had to do as they were told, and I suppose it was something different! Any bus trip had novelty value for us, and on one of the comforts stops we might be lucky enough to score an ice-cream cone.

In summertime, Mrs Perkins organised a seaside trip to Skegness or Hunstanton, which were located either side of the Wash. A day out like this took a fair bit of planning.

The weather had to be considered, so you might set off in a summer dress, but don't forget your cardigan and mackintosh because the weather could change dramatically throughout the day. Then there was the question of food and drink. Lots of sandwiches, of course, more rock cakes and jam tarts. Bottles of weak cordial for the children, bottles of cold sweet milky tea for the adults and perhaps a thermos of Camp coffee for the sophisticates. Throw in a few towels just in case anyone got really wet and for sitting on the sand.

We eagerly anticipated those days, but the state of the tides never seemed to vary much. The sea seemed to be far off near to the horizon, so it was a long walk just for a paddle, then the water was usually quite cold and uninviting.

I don't remember anyone getting wet all over—the most I ever managed was a paddle up to the knees, which was enough.

The town behind the beach didn't have much to offer either. These trips were just after the war had ended and the beaches had been cleared of concrete bastions and wire to prevent invasion by landing craft. There were a few souvenir shops selling seaside rocks with the name of the town on them, as well as postcards with lots of fat ladies on them.

There were also cafés for those who had not brought enough food from home. On the comfort stop on the way home, those not wishing to go to the toilet might return to the bus with newspaper packets of fish and chips, so we would spend the rest of the journey with the tantalising smell of vinegary chips throughout the bus.

There was also the annual trip to the pantomime at the theatre in Peterborough after Christmas. This was doubly exciting as it meant we went out after dark, something we very rarely did being children of the blackout era.

Dozens of coaches unloaded their cargoes of eager children and parents, all intent on getting into the theatre as fast as possible to find out where they were sitting. Gazing around at the theatrical splendour of the place and all those people was a real treat!

Connie and I never left our seats during the interval; I think she thought we would never find them again, besides which she had limited what I drank all day, so I didn't need to 'go.'

After the performance there was always a mad rush to get outside and find our bus amongst all the others lined up outside the theatre. We would all sing one of the catchy tunes from the show on the bus ride home.

The war ended in 1945, so November 5 that year was the first-time people lit bonfires and burned effigies of Guy Fawkes. In previous years, showing a light after dark was an offence.

Someone in a yard farther down the street lit a large bonfire and everyone was invited. There were no fireworks as such, and the adults poked large potatoes into the ashes to cook while we children raced around the fire and yelled and screamed when the figure of Guy Fawkes, a scarecrow, fell into the flames. There must have been other bonfire nights after that, but that first one has always stayed in my memory.

RABBITS AND DONUTS

OTHER EVENTS OF A LESS ORGANISED NATURE included rabbit drives. One side of the village had a very large rabbit warren through the fields, and every now and then Mr Fay, the village shop owner, organised the event.

Every young lad and his dog and any able-bodied men that were available took part. There were also a couple of men who brought their ferrets along, but they usually kept a bit apart from the rest of us. I was very keen to see a ferret, and one of the men brought his out of his pocket when I asked, but he did warn me that they had very sharp teeth and fingers were something they liked a lot. That was enough for me to keep my hands in my pockets.

The drive involved the lads leading their dogs to burrows that were obviously in use. The dogs would bark loudly, and the smaller ones would try to dig into the burrow. All the noise and commotion were meant to drive the rabbits to an exit burrow or two where wire netting had been placed and held firm with stakes.

As the rabbits exited in fright, they would be caught by the netting, and someone would hit them on the head to kill them. They were gutted on the spot, then hung on poles to be taken back to the shed behind the shop where they would be skinned.

This was not deemed a fitting occupation for girls, of course, but I badgered to be allowed to go see what happened. Eventually I wore the opposition down and was allowed to go.

I was told I wouldn't like it and would have to find my own way home. Well, I didn't like it much, but I was not going to admit it. I went several times. I was given a stout stick and told to hit the rabbits hard on the head. I liked rabbits, so it was difficult for me to be so violent to them.

At the same time, there was usually such a heaving mass of them, and I knew that any human hand trying to rescue them would be badly bitten, so I clobbered them, and it was all over quickly for each one.

The boys resented me in the beginning, but when they saw I could do it they decided to have competitions with me on the side. We children didn't have any involvement in the gutting process, but I earned the title of the fastest rabbit skinner of the district. I could defrock a bunny faster than the rest.

The carcases were then put in boxes, and Mr Fay took them away. Later, I learnt that he took them to a camp of Polish soldiers just outside the village.

Unlike the American soldiers, they did not have a plentiful supply of food.

However, they did have some supplies from the American troops, and sometimes word would go out that there were 'donuts tonight.' We may not have had much in the way of telephones, but the grapevine flourished.

Around 7:00 pm with hat, coat, and gloves on, I would set off for the shed behind the shop. I also had a shilling inside one glove. I ventured into the shed through two horse blankets that were thrown over the door and waited my turn.

Visitors slid between the door blankets so that no chink of light escaped during the black out, and for quite a while after the end of the war people were still rather wary of showing a light at night.

Mr Fay would be busy frying the donuts, and his wife rolled them in sugar and put them into poke bags made from greaseproof paper. She took the money as she handed them over. As the shop had all our ration books, they knew how many mouths there were in each family. We were allowed one donut per person, and they were threepence each. I collected three in a bag and received threepence change. I then raced home to eat mine in front of the fire with a mug of cocoa.

THE HARVEST FESTIVAL

I WAS IN THE RIGHT PLACE AT THE RIGHT TIME to enjoy the annual Harvest Festival celebrations for several years. The main celebration was always held on a Thursday evening with a slightly less fervent service on the following Sunday. Later in life I learnt that in some circles such festivals were considered semi-pagan and there wasn't much allowance for them in the regular church calendar.

Our house was on the road to the church, and a procession of people went past throughout the day taking their offerings there.

Big baskets of garden produce and fruit, fresh butter, cheeses, sheaves of oats and wheat, freshly baked loaves of bread plaited in the shape of corn sheaves and masses of flowers of all descriptions.

My aunt picked her Michaelmas daisies early in the day and stored them in the washhouse to keep them fresh.

One of my jobs was to polish the apples that were to accompany the jars of preserved fruit and homemade jams and jellies that we took up to the church in the afternoon.

The whole grey interior of the place was transformed with the corn sheaves tied to the pillars, fruit and flowers in every nook and cranny. Despite the war and food rationing in the country, there was always ways of siphoning off some food, such as milk and eggs to make butter and cheese. The butter being offered was homemade and the best quality.

Attendance at the Thursday evening service rivalled Easter and Christmas with many of the farming families making their annual visit and others who rarely darkened the church doorways except for weddings, christenings and funerals also joining us for the night.

It was often a tight squeeze in the pews, but at least we smaller fry couldn't slip off the polished seats as we gazed at all this wonderful bounty. We knew we would be robbing God if we helped ourselves even to the smallest apple.

The traditional harvest hymns were sung with enough gusto to disturb the dust motes on the high beams. The choir was always augmented for this service by noted singers from the local Methodist chapel, and we always sang a rousing anthem after the sermon. After the service it was time for the congregation to process around the church, with many commenting on the size or beauty or the generosity of some donations.

My main interest was to find the 'corn dollies.' These were always to be found at the back of the church by the old stone font. They were made each year by two women who lived on an outlying farm.

They never attended church but sent their creations, together with a handsome financial contribution. In later years when a new rector took over, he took exception to the dollies, labelling them as pagan symbols, so no more dollies appeared. The parish was poorer for that too.

My aunt would be in a hurry to get home and lay out the supper she had prepared for all our visitors, but I could usually persuade her to let me stay in the care of another courtesy aunt.

This aunt knew many people who did not appear in my aunt's circle of friends, and they exchanged news and gossip as we wended our way down the churchyard path. As you may have been told, 'little pigs have big ears,' and I know I was privy to some items of gossip that only made sense years later.

When we arrived home, the kettle would be boiling, and supper laid out. This was also the night when the latest batch of elderberry wine was tasted. If I was lucky, I was given a sip before I was sent up to bed. I've no idea who made the wine or what happened to the rest of it, but it certainly never appeared in our house except for that evening.

I went back to the village about forty years ago and happened to be there for that year's Harvest Festival, so I went along. What a difference!

There were no sheaves of corn around the pillars, and although the flowers were nice, there was nowhere near the abundance as in my childhood.

When it came to the produce, some vegetables and fruits were prepackaged, and I saw mostly store-bought jams. Surprisingly, there were a few tins of dog and cat food included.

By then, the village didn't have its own cleric, he was visiting only. True to form, the congregation sat toward the back, so he had to persuade us to move forward. The organ had died several years earlier, but an old lady who I recognized as the mother of one of my school friends played a very old harmonium which gave more wheeze than music.

We sang the harvest hymns as well as we could, but it was very muted compared to previous memories. After the service we walked down toward the churchyard gate, the church door was locked, and everyone got into their cars and were gone. Such a contrast. My aunt wanted to know all about it, but I hadn't the heart to describe such a non-event in detail, so I launched into 'Do you remember when...,' and in no time we were both back in the good old days.

MOTOTCYCLE DAYS

Uncle Bob and his friend Dennis would sometimes head off together on their motorbikes to a racing venue not too far away. At one time, Dennis had a bike with a sidecar, and they decided I was about the right size and weight to be the sidecar passenger in some races. No special leathers in those days. Both myself and Dennis would be wrapped in newspaper under our clothes as insulation against the cold and hopefully protection if we had a mishap. I quite enjoyed it and quickly learnt how to lean into the bends as required. I think I grew too large to fit in the sidecar after two seasons, but Dennis had bought himself another motorcycle anyway.

BURIAL RITES

DEATHS IN THE VILLAGE HAD THEIR OWN RITUALS regardless of religious calling. When someone was ailing to the point of death, members of the family would take turns staying with that person so they would not be alone when the grim reaper called. The village rector would also call to lend his prayers and spiritual support to the family and suggest a time for someone to discuss funeral arrangements with him. Apart from a few families who attended the Methodist Chapel in the village, which employed a visiting minister, I don't think any other denominations were represented in the village.

Meantime, enquiries would have been made as to where 'the door' was located. This was a solid wooden door on which the dead body would be laid after it had been ritually washed and then dressed in whatever was chosen to be worn in the coffin. This was done by close family members or the district nurse.

I have no idea of the origin of this door, but between uses it was usually stored at the Sexton's house. The door would be placed on top of a table in the deceased's house, the dressed body laid upon it and covered by a thin sheet. Members of the family would take turns staying there until the body was placed in the coffin.

Soon after the death, the local carpenter would call at the house armed with his tape measure to determine the size of the coffin to be prepared. The rest of the village took it upon themselves to provide the grieving family with ready-cooked meals and sustenance, and the local grave diggers would be hard at work in the churchyard.

In those days there were no mechanical diggers. A spade and mattock job and if there been little rain for a while, very hard work.

On the day of the funeral, the windows of all the houses lining the street leading to the churchyard would all have their curtains drawn as a mark of respect.

If the funeral was for someone of standing in the village, people not of the immediate family would stand in the street with heads bowed—men with hats or caps off—then they would often peel off the pavements and join the funeral procession.

The food for the wake or post-funeral gathering was provided by friends and neighbours, and some ladies always provided the same dish, rather like a party piece. Connie could usually be relied upon to provide a tray of parkin, a particular kind of shortbread.

Sometimes for years after the funeral, a member of the family would visit the churchyard once a week to make sure the grave was kept neat and tidy, flowers renewed, grass clipped, and headstone scrubbed if it showed signs of lichen growth.

These patterns evolved over time, and there were times when a visit to the churchyard was almost a social occasion, with villagers meeting while tending their relatives. That churchyard has been closed to new burials, and with the modern tendency toward cremation, visiting a memorial wall doesn't have quite the same appeal.

TEMPTATIONS ABOUND

As I mentioned earlier, I moved several times during my early childhood. Sometimes I stayed with real aunts, and other times I went with 'courtesy aunts.' I began school when I was four and a half years old. By this time, I could read quite well and knew how to count, so I began school life in the second class.

I think some of the temporary moves were triggered by my naughtiness and Connie not really knowing how to cope with such behaviour. I'll admit that I did get up to mischief quite often.

Sunday trading was Not Done in the 1940s. For some reason beyond my understanding, the village shop did open on Sunday afternoons for a few weeks for one summer. It might have been for the convenience of some American soldiers billeted outside the village.

My friend Margaret and I noticed it when we took her little dog for a walk after Sunday School one week. The next week I persuaded Margaret to keep her collection penny instead of putting it in the plate. I did likewise. After Sunday School, we collected her little dog, went into the shop, pooled our pennies, and bought a water ice on a stick. Then we climbed over a wall into a farmyard opposite and shared this delicious treat between us before taking the dog for a further walk and then home. However, on the third week, we had just finished our feast when it began to teem with rain, so we rushed back to my home (which was closest) for shelter.

We didn't have to say a word as both of us had purple mouths and tongues from the dye used in the icy poles. This dye had disappeared during our walk on previous weeks. Margaret was sent home, and I was told off in no uncertain manner. A bit later, my aunt went over to Margaret's house to speak to her mother.

The next Sunday, both Connie and Mrs H came to Sunday School with us. The rector gave a short talk after the hymns about the sin of stealing. Then he asked if any of us had been guilty of such a thing.

Of course, Margaret and I had our arms raised by the adults, and we had to confess that we had been stealing from God Himself!

It was so unfair as there were several others in the congregation who were just as guilty, but we already knew that if you 'dobbed' you were marked for life. The adults then went into the vestry to confer. In our minds the vestry was where God lived, so it was very serious.

The punishment meted out was that both of us must go to the rectory garden for four Saturday mornings to do weeding. Our hearts sank into our boots as weeding was very difficult. We were never sure which was weed, and which was plant, so it was going to be four Saturdays of purgatory.

However, when we arrived the next week, we found that the whole of the garden we were to tackle was filled to the brim with sour thistles only. It was a matter of pull as many as you can!

Looking back on that escapade, I remember that it was a walled garden with old fruit trees espaliered on two of the walls and a rather ornate bird bath in one corner. The rector's sister came out during the morning and fed us milk and seed cake.

We explained to her that sour thistles were prime rabbit food, and we knew lots of people who would love to have some. By the end of the morning, she had borrowed someone's little cart and she helped us put our weeds into bundles. Then we set off round the village selling our bundles to those keeping rabbits. We made enough money to repay God and had a little left over to buy ourselves an icy pole each, but not on a Sunday.

MORE MISCHIEF

One day, I heard Connie and Bob discussing sending me for a short break to stay with Aunt Ethel, another of my father's sisters. They mentioned the fact that Ethel's son was a real terror and wondered how I would get along with him.

I had no idea what 'a real terror' was, but I didn't think I would like it, so I wasn't all that keen to go.

The day dawned and I was put on the train, in the guard's van as usual. At that time, it was quite common to send unaccompanied children in care of the train guard so long as the child was wearing a label with the vital statistics on it: name, age, destination, etc. Sometimes there were interesting parcels travelling in the van that I would observe and spend time wondering what they might contain. There might be trays of day-old chicks, and one time there had been a nanny goat tied up in one corner.

This trip didn't have any such distractions. I asked permission to go to the toilet. When I had finished, instead of going back to the guard's van, I turned the other way and started to explore the train.

I came across a carriage bursting with children all about my age and very excited. They were going on holiday to the seaside. There were a couple of adults, and I heard one of the children ask a question to 'Miss Brown,' so I asked her who Miss Brown was. She was one of the helpers at the place where they lived.

I was still there when the train stopped at a station, and we all got out and went across the platform to another train that was waiting there.

A holiday at the seaside sounded much better than facing a 'real terror.' After another short train ride, we were all herded onto a bus and taken to the camp that was going to be our home for the holiday.

There was a large, long hut for the girls, and a similar one for the boys. No one seemed to count heads during all of this, so I just went with the flow. I had removed my label and invented a name for myself, Felicity. I had a lovely three days at the beach before I was found and handed over to a policeman.

He gave me quite a telling off, but I tried to look suitably sorry, so he bought me an ice-cream during the trip. I ate my treat and chatted about some of the things I'd done while at the seaside.

Aunt Ethel had met the train, but the guard who was meant to watch me had to take over another guard's van at short notice and had left the station. When he wasn't there to be questioned, Aunt Ethel presumed I must have been sick and not travelled that day, so she sent a telegram to Connie to ask when she might expect me to arrive.

That was when the balloon went up. Someone remembered the children going on holiday, and that's how I was traced. I was left in no doubt as to how much worry I had caused, and no further trips were planned for a long while.

Another real aunt was Aunt Lily, one of my mother's sisters. She and her husband lived on a small farm in another village together with their two children. Both John and Mary were a bit older than me, but when I was there, we all went along to the local primary school. I quite liked going there as Aunt Lily did not seem to have any hard and fast rules about a lot of things.

If we'd had several days of gloomy weather and then a day dawned when the sun shone and the birds sang, at breakfast Aunt Lily might say that it looked like a lovely day for a picnic! In next to no time a basket would be packed with sandwiches and apples, and the four of us would take off across fields and through little woods until we found a place that looked good for exploring.

She never seemed to mind if we got a bit wet in streams or got mud on our clothes. She would join in our games and later in the day we'd all troop home very tired but with lots of nice memories of the day.

The farm had cows, pigs, hens, and some cattle in fields, and I think Uncle Horace grew corn or barley too. This was during the war, and I understood that the government knew just how many of everything they had on the farm, and all produce had to be sent to factories or somewhere to be counted and shared. All milk was to go in the large churn that was left by the farm gate, and all eggs apart from the cracked ones, went to the egg marketing board.

Somehow, a large bowl of milk would always be left in the larder, Aunt Lily would 'trip' with the basket of eggs so that those eggs could be counted as cracked.

There was no TV in those days, so long winter evenings could be spent churning the cream that was skimmed from the bowl of milk into butter. Some of this, plus many supposedly cracked eggs were then taken by the three of us round the village to old people.

THE SPARE PIG

With regards to the extra piglet, that hadn't been counted when they were born, it grew along with the rest, but the grapevine in the village was very much alive to the presence or otherwise of ministry inspectors. Uncle Horace had contingency plans in place for this. If ministry men were in the area, Aunt Lily would get on her bicycle, pedal to the school, have a quick word with the teacher and we three children would be excused.

We would take off across the fields carrying the basket that Aunt had brought to the school, to a pre-planned spot in the corner of a field. The spare pig would be enclosed behind straw bundles, and our job was to keep it quiet by feeding it small apples and scratching its back with sticks. If we sighted officials who looked as though they were heading our way, I was to be thrown into the stream that ran down the next hedgerow so my screams would deflect attention.

If I wasn't staying there, Mary was to provide the diversion in a similar fashion. We never had to put it into practice, but it provided a deal of excitement.

I was at the farm one year when it was time to kill the spare pig. We children were allowed to take our supper upstairs that evening, something not usually done. We ate that quickly then crept to the bathroom which overlooked the close yard. The bathroom had a long window high in the end wall, and we had to stand on the rim of the bath to see out.

All the neighbours came along to help, bringing their knives and basins with them. The poor pig was dragged into the yard, squealing loudly; then there was a dull thud—the stun gun. Then the pig's throat was cut, the blood collected, and the job of butchering began.

Later, there were sounds of great activity in the kitchen below and smells of cooking, rendering the fat from beneath the pig's skin.

It was nothing to find sides of curing bacon hanging in the most unusual places throughout the year. During the autumn and winter, my aunt and uncle would help in the same process in other farm kitchens, and we would receive a cut of fresh pork to be cooked at home. There must have been a roster amongst all the small farms as to who killed when, and, depending on which farm they had been to, the 'payment' of a piece of pork varied.

I'm sure the ministry men were aware of all these clandestine activities and scored a few pork chops and extra eggs at times.

PLYMOUTH AND ROBERT

My own brush with the war came when I was sent to stay with a couple who lived in Cornwall. This was in May 1944, and I was just over six years old.

Plymouth was heavily bombed, especially the dockyard areas, but parts of the town were pretty badly damaged too. The event I record here was likely during the last bombing raids in that area.

I had been there once before and loved it. Aunt Beth's husband had been at college with my mother's cousin, Eric. This and the time before were the only times my mother's side of the family, apart from Aunt Lily, had any contact with me until many years later.

When I was in my mid-forties, I visited Cousin Eric and had lunch at his home. By then he was very old, but he was able to fill in some of the blanks in my knowledge about my mother's family. Apparently, he had kept track of my life throughout, and he wished to meet me again before he died.

He arranged my travel to Cornwall, and it was he who later arranged for me to be put into the Catholic girls' boarding school after the Plymouth tragedy.

It was arranged that I would be put on the train from Peterborough down to King's Cross Station in London. Cousin Eric took me to Paddington Station where he left me in the charge of the train guard for the train trip to Plymouth.

Aunt Beth collected me when I arrived in Plymouth, and we took the ferry across the river Tamar. We then went to a stable, collected the pony and trap, and we were off down several winding lanes to a small village about five miles from the ferry.

She and her husband didn't have any family of their own, but when I visited this time, they had an evacuee from the East End of London staying there. Robert was just under a year older than me, but this was his first taste of country life.

I took great delight in showing him where milk and eggs came from. Of course, this was all very strange to him as was the vegetable garden and fruit orchard.

When I first arrived, we both attended the local village school. We caught chickenpox at the same time, which meant we had to stay home while we were still spotty. One day, Aunt Beth had several errands to do in Plymouth, so we all went there in the pony and trap over the river on the ferry.

We walked into town, and Aunt Beth asked us to go and collect some boots that had been put in for mending. Robert had been with her when she had taken the boots in, so he knew the way. Then we were to meet her at the chemist shop while she did some of the other things on her list.

Robert and I collected the boots and were walking down Armada Way, a very wide street. I was carrying the boots when Robert suddenly pushed me so hard that I stumbled up some steps and into a shop doorway. I fell forward onto the boots and managed to scrape both knees and bite my lip.

He landed on top of me. When I got my breath back, I began to shout at him to get off me, but he didn't move. When I wriggled out from under, I realised he was dead. The back of his head was covered in blood.

I was completely stunned by the turn of events and began to cry loudly. People came out of the shop to see what all the noise was about, and they were all horrified.

Eventually, I was taken to the chemist shop, Aunt Beth was found and given the news about Robert. I think someone took us down to the ferry, and we collected the pony and trap on the other side of the river and set off for home. The pony knew the way, of course, which was just as well as both of us cried the whole way.

Later that evening, the village policeman visited the farm to let Aunt Beth know that Robert had been killed by bullets fired from a German plane on its way back across the Channel. It was thought that he may have recognised the whine of the plane as it came in to fire its last bullets. Strafing the streets was common if planes had ammunition left over.

I remained at the farm for a while after that, and Aunt Beth did her best to keep me busy helping her around the house and letting me help with the cooking. She did her best to assure me that Robert was now in heaven, but my faith in God was severely shaken. I wasn't sure I wanted to believe in God when he allowed such things to happen.

One day a telegram arrived, and I was taken to Plymouth the next day, put on a train in the guard's van again, met by Cousin Eric at Paddington Station, then onto yet another train to Cambridge.

Cousin Eric travelled with me and said he had arranged for me to go to a safe place for a while. At the end of the school term, I would be going home to Connie and Bob. The reasoning behind all this movement was far beyond my understanding, but he was an adult so was supposed to know what was best.

A nun was on the platform waiting for our train, so I said goodbye to Cousin Eric, and the nun took me with her to a girls' boarding home run by the Catholic nuns. My arrival at the home was in the middle of their school term and, as I did not have a Catholic upbringing, I was always putting my foot in it when it came to the rituals of such a place.

Sister Eucharia was given the task of trying to keep me on the straight and narrow as it were, but I think she found me very trying.

She impressed upon me that everyone had a guardian angel sitting on their left shoulder. He saw and heard everything, and even knew my thoughts, implying that they had all better be pure.

When she was particularly vexed with me, she would keep saying, 'You should make more visits my child.' I had no idea what she was talking about, but I thought she may be referring to the fact that I was very constipated and should visit the toilet more often.

How could I explain to her that having an angel on my shoulder all the time was very inhibiting to performing well in the toilet?

I was in my mid-forties before I discovered the meaning of her words. A friend with a good Catholic upbringing was visiting, and she said something about 'visits,' so I asked her to explain. She related a time during her childhood when she had done something that was considered naughty, and she knew the nuns would find out about it sooner or later.

Making visits was when you went to church when it was not a proper service time and you had a quiet word with God, explaining your side of the story before the nuns spoke to Him about your behaviour.

At the end of that school term, I was put on a train and collected at the end of my journey by Aunt Mary, whom my eldest sister was living with. These few days were the only ones when I met up with my eldest sister during my childhood, so she remained a virtual stranger from then on.

I stayed with her and her husband much later when I was on one of my return visits to the UK, and I was rather mystified by the way she cleaned every surface possible with bleach. I wondered if she sanitised the whole house after I left.

A few days with my sister at Aunt Mary's and it was back to Connie and Bob in my own village. They must have known what had happened during my time away, but it was never mentioned, and I settled back into life, seemingly unchanged.

I was visiting England many years later after I had emigrated to Australia, and I had the opportunity to revisit Aunt Beth down in Cornwall. She told me Robert's elder brother visited her about ten years after his death to thank her.

He let her know that both their parents had been killed in an air raid, and he had been brought up by their grandmother. It was on this visit to England that I had lunch with Cousin Eric, too, which helped me sort out that chaotic time of my childhood in my mind.

VILLAGE SCHOOL

Miss Bonner oversaw the infant school and ran both classes with the assistance of a Miss Smart. Miss Bonner was a very tall woman and was 'well covered,' as it was described in those days. She lived at the end of the village with her elderly mother, wore National Health framed spectacles and taught at Sunday School. National Health was the government-run scheme whereby mothers of babies could receive concentrated orange juice for the infants.

Primary school children all received a third of a pint of milk each school day. Also included in this was the provision of school doctors who checked the overall health of the growing children and, due to my short sightedness, I was allocated spectacles with the familiar black metal frames. I realise now that I was very fortunate to have my lack of focus discovered at such an early age.

All lessons were held in the one large room with a coke stove in the middle to warm the place in winter. The place filled with fumes sometimes. In the second class we were allowed to try our hand using pen and ink.

This was where we learnt our multiplication tables by rote. Educators of today scoff at such methods, but I would hazard a guess that most of us who attended those classes can still recite our tables, do mental arithmetic, and mentally work out how much change we should be given when shopping.

There were two toilet blocks, one for girls and one for boys, with toilets like those at our homes. They smelled dreadful.

During primary schooling in the village, all the children went home for their lunch. Most of the mothers worked at home to clean, feed and clothe their families and help grow vegetables and keep chickens; they wouldn't have had time for full-time outside employment.

Boys and girls all raced around together in the playground. When we moved to what was called the 'big school,' the different genders played in different yards. The top school was a more modern building with three school rooms. The first was taught by Mrs Perkins. She must have been in her late forties when I was in her class.

She was not very tall, rather rotund, with hair in a bun and no nonsense in her room, but we liked her because she made the lessons interesting. She lived in a large house next door to my friend Margaret, and I used to walk her little terrier dog each Sunday when I was in my teens. She was also a useful safety valve for me. She was aware of the lack of relationship between myself and Connie, and I found I could ask her questions I knew Connie would never answer.

The middle room was taught by Miss Smitheringale. I knew she had a hard life at times because she had a younger brother who suffered from Down syndrome. Village children only knew him as that boy they all called names and teased whenever they had a chance.

Teddy never attended school, but during his teens a variety of people employed him to tend their gardens and he made a life for himself working this way.

The third room was taught by Mr Tillson. He was the headmaster and supervised the playground activities on important national days. I remember that on Empire Day we all stood in line at attention as the flag was raised, then we sang the national anthem. One boy, who was an evacuee from Poland living with relatives in the village, refused to salute the flag and sing, and there was quite a fuss about that.

I never progressed further than Mrs Perkins as I was given the opportunity to sit the dreaded eleven plus exam a year before I was expected to.

The morning Mr Tillson was notified I had passed and been offered a scholarship to go to the girls' high school in Stamford, he came to the classroom to give me and Mrs Perkins the news. He suggested I might like to run home and tell my aunt.

When I arrived at the cottage, Connie was black leading the grate and very surprised to see me at that time in the morning. When I gave her the news, she just said, 'Well, that's nice. Now hurry back to school, you're missing lessons.' It was quite deflating for me, but with hindsight, I think her first thought must have been in relation to the extra expense this promotion meant.

I know that when my father visited us there were discussions relating to his non-contribution to my welfare, and I also know that he always had an excuse as to why he couldn't contribute.

My father only visited us about once a year, always on a Sunday when he knew he would get a roast dinner. I would be told that my father was coming, but he was a rather strange man who had a moustache and smelt of snuff, and I had no idea what feelings I was supposed to have for him.

When it was time for him to leave, he would jingle the change in his trouser pocket, and if I was lucky, I got two shillings and sixpence, or else just two shillings. He didn't approve of secondary education for girls, but, fortunately for we three girls, our carers did. Seeing that he didn't contribute to my upkeep anyway, it really didn't affect him at all.

HIGH SCHOOL

CONNIE AND I WERE SUMMONED to the school for an interview with the head mistress. She was an imposing figure, rather mannish in the way she dressed, but she had a twinkle in her eye, and I came to appreciate her style of management throughout my years there.

There was only one shop in town that sold the requisite uniform clothing, but Bob's niece had attended the school several years before me, so I scored her winter and Panama hats and hockey stick. Connie bought me a new leather satchel, which I loved. Whenever I smell new leather, it reminds me of the way I felt about that bag.

Each intake was divided into three streams, and I remained in the first stream all through my time there. This streaming was designed to place the brighter students in the first stream while those in the third took general classes and were taught basic cookery and sewing.

There were times when I would have liked to join the third stream. Although Connie was a very good cook, she was also impatient when it came to teaching me.

I was either too ham-fisted or too slow. About the only job she thought I did well was grating the large block of cooking salt to fill the pot of salt she kept on the stovetop.

Our first English teacher taught us to appreciate language and introduced us to Shakespeare through glimpses of the way life was lived while he was writing. It helped me understand his writing more. I found Latin very interesting, too, as our teacher illustrated how many modern words were derived from old Latin. I still enjoy exploring derivations. A French Madame taught French in what I always thought of as the garden room. It had large bay windows that looked out onto the lawns and garden, and there was a nice atmosphere no matter the weather outside. It helped that Madame made learning fun.

My classmates were a motley crew. A few were from the town schools, but the rest of us hailed from a variety of towns and villages over quite a large radius. This meant everyone had to find new friends.

I gravitated to a group of social misfits. At break times, we five were not interested in discussing boys or fashion. Instead, we gravitated to a spot in front of the bicycle sheds to share views and information, usually concerning some recent lessons. We only met during school hours because we lived so far from each other.

I think we were all a bit mystified by Rachel; her family were part of the local Plymouth Brethren, a rather strict religious sect.

No TV, only listened to the news on the wireless, no cinema, or theatres. I don't think any of us indulged in those diversions much, but I couldn't imagine a life where none of that was allowed.

However, Rachel had a delightful sense of humour and was considered very bright. Pepita was joined by her younger sister the following year, and these girls were very serious scholars. They travelled from Oundle, quite a distance, where their father was a senior master at Oundle School.

This was one of the noted boys' schools after Eton, Harrow, Rugby, Westminster and Uppingham. Sheena was a Canadian lass. Her father was some important brass at Cottesmore Airfield, so her primary schooling had all been in Canada. The other member of our group was Ursula; she had grown up in Holland, so Dutch was her native language. Her parents, teachers at Uppingham, were bilingual, and her English was perfect.

When I was around twelve years old the house that Bob had been born in was renovated, and we moved there to live. This meant that I had a bedroom of my own.

Nice I suppose, but in those days, bedrooms were only for sleeping and this one was so bitterly cold during winter it was a case of dive under the blankets and hug the hot water bottle.

I think it was during my second year there that I began to menstruate. At that time there was almost nothing available for young girls to read concerning this, and I'd gleaned most of my information from overheard conversations in the cloakroom when we were hanging up coats or changing shoes.

On my eventful day, I went downstairs in the morning and told Connie that I had made a bit of a mess in the bed. I knew what it signified, but it was not a topic that had ever been raised at home, and I didn't feel comfortable enough to ask Connie.

At my news she remarked that she had been expecting this to happen. She took me back upstairs, went to the bottom drawer of the big chest in my bedroom, brought out a packet of pads and the necessary belt, showed me how to assemble and wear, advised me as to how I was to wrap the used articles and where to put them for later burning under the copper.

'From now on, don't let any boys touch you!' she concluded.

That was the extent of her explanation. Why or how boys might want to touch me was never explained.

I remember the embarrassment when buying packets of pads. Even in Woolworth stores, goods for sale were displayed on the counter, but the assistant would have to put it in a bag and take the money. I would blush bright red if the assistant happened to be a man. It was a similar situation at the chemist shop too.

Later that year, at speech day when parents could meet teachers, the gym mistress asked Connie to find me a brassiere to wear please.

Connie never wore a bra, but she never wore dresses that needed such underpinnings either. However, she took me shopping, and I was properly fitted and taught how to don the garment.

By the time I reached the end of my fifth year and could have left school, but I was offered a place in the lower sixth. I had already decided I wanted to be a nurse, but training didn't start until I was eighteen years old, so I was allowed to stay for the extra year.

My choice of nursing was not stimulated by thoughts of wiping the fevered brow, but I knew that during training, nurses were required to live at the hospital and trainees were paid too.

The school offered a course on human biology in this final year, and Connie encouraged me to do it. She may have thought it would explain human development in a way that would make up for her lack of knowledge or ability to explain the facts of life to me.

None of that was forthcoming, although we did learn about cells, nuclei, and bacteria, which were all useful later. We spent most of our time examining the inner workings of the frog, including a couple of sessions dissecting one. I also studied a little ancient Greek that year as well as more Latin.

My main delight were the days that we spent in the art room. It was full of weird and wonderful objects for still-life compositions, and the art teacher allowed free expression in whatever medium you chose. Absolutely liberating, and probably sewed the seed for my later creativity.

During my last two years at school, I did a newspaper delivery round in the village six days a week and received six shillings for my trouble. I pedalled around on my bicycle and, apart from winter mornings which could be bitterly cold and wet, I enjoyed having the streets to myself. The money I earned was the first pocket money I'd ever had.

School finished for the year at the end of July, so I had about four months to wait until my nursing course began. There was very little in the way of job opportunities. I did not have any clerical skills, and counter assistants who lived near to the place of employment stood a better chance of getting those jobs than I did, living in a village with no reliable transport.

To keep me out of mischief, Connie tasked me with more chores around the house as she had found herself a job in a school canteen where they produced a hot lunch for all the children. Once my chores were done, I was free to please myself. Most days I was off into the fields and woods all around, observing all kinds of interesting things. I knew where a local vixen was hiding her cubs and where the first spring flowers would appear.

There was a very large oak tree on a hillside, and I found I could climb to a good height along the branches. This gave me a sweeping view of the wide valley, and I spent hours perched up there just observing.

I noticed a group of boys, sort of lurking in the bushes a few times. They were quiet and seemed to be doing things with a purpose. My curiosity kept me watching, and one day I decided to watch them from ground level. I was a little careless and stepped on a twig that snapped loudly, so I was discovered. I was taken to their leader, a fellow probably in his early 20s. I didn't know the boys and I presumed they lived in Stamford. The leader had what I now recognise as an Irish accent, and they all referred to each other by number, not names! After a bit of questioning, they asked if I would like to join them. I became number 17—but keep it secret! OK by me.

MISCHIEF GALORE

IT WAS A WHOLE NEW WORLD. We learnt how to manufacture good Molotov cocktails, not that we ever did, but we did practice our hurling techniques. Molotov cocktails were otherwise known as 'poor man's grenades.' They were made by filling glass bottles with petrol, stuffing the neck with an old rag and lighting it just before you hurled it at the target.

I also learnt handy skills such as how to handle sticks of gelignite and attach detonators and where to place them for maximum effect on such things as a railway bridge. We also learnt a bit about TNT, and even got to feel what we were told was some Semtex!

Another handy skill was the ability to pick locks. This was before the advent of plastic credit cards which could also be used in this fashion.

Fortunately for me, the village policeman was also observing this group. He recognised me as a village girl, as he and Bob were avid potato growers who tried out all kinds of new varieties.

He called in to visit Bob and Connie and had a long talk with them. Then I was invited into the sitting room to be included in the discussion. The policeman had only reported the leader and the boys to higher authorities, but there was a chance they may mention a female accomplice when they were rounded up. He was sure that if charges were laid, they would be very serious. In view of this, he thought it was a good idea if I left the village for a while.

Connie and Bob were completely stunned. They had no idea I had been mixed up in such things. The next morning, Connie sent a telegram to her eldest sister, Ethel, saying she would telephone her that evening and could she ask her husband Wilfred to be there for consultation. I was not allowed to stray outside the garden the next day,

Connie took me with her to the public phone by the post office in the evening. Making a long- distance phone call was quite a challenge for her. This was probably only the second time she had done such a thing, but we got it right between us. She pressed button A and found herself talking to Ethel. She explained the situation as best she could, and then I was allowed to speak to Aunt Ethel with my side of the story.

Connie then asked whether Uncle Wilfred could think of any way to help me disappear for a while. By now we had used our allotted time, so Connie agreed we would be at the phone box the next evening for advice on the matter.

Another day confined to the garden, then another trip to the telephone box. This time we waited for the telephone to ring. Connie picked up the receiver to find Wilfred speaking to her. She made notes on the back of an envelope in her bag, repeated some of the instructions back to Wilfred, then had a short chat with Ethel.

On the way home, Connie informed me I would be going by train the next day and I must do everything Uncle Wilfred asked me to do if I wanted to keep out of trouble. As far as I knew, Uncle Wilfred taught at a boys' school, was a lay preacher and organist at his Methodist church, and at one time had owned a boat. In view of the way he organised my disappearance, I have often wondered who else he worked for and what other attributes he had.

All of this remains a mystery even today as by the time I began to think about this episode in my life, all of those who were involved were either dead or lost to the world. All these repercussions from what had seemed to me to be an interesting interlude. I also received quite a talking to that left me in no doubt that I was in serious trouble, so don't rock the boat.

I packed a small case that night, and our neighbour drove the two of us to Peterborough railway station the next day where I was put aboard the London train in the charge of the guard. When we arrived at King's Cross Station, Uncle Wilfred was there to meet me.

He whisked me to Paddington Station, and before I had time to think, we were both aboard the *Cornish Express.* We shared the sandwiches that Connie had given me. But Wilfred didn't really explain where we were going or why, just that it was for my own good. We eventually arrived at Falmouth.

Down to the harbour and we were looking for a particular boat. It turned out to be a large cruising yacht. On board, Uncle Wilfred told me I would be joining the crew and he was sure I would enjoy the experience.

He went to speak with the captain while I was led below decks and shown where I would be sleeping.

I was completely stunned by all of this and didn't argue. Perhaps I should explain that even though I was a very naïve teenage girl, I really didn't have much going for me by way of feminine attraction. I was rather tubby with no discernible curves, straight hair, and spectacles with National Health frames.

The crew were a mix of Spanish, French and Greek, and I ended up really enjoying the trip. We sailed on the night tide and spent the entire trip polishing and scrubbing the ship from top to bottom. She was being ferried back to Marseilles after some sort of repairs had been done. The captain was the only one onboard who spoke English well.

As I had no papers or identification, I was also shown how to disappear into a rather tight sail locker if we were boarded by officials, and I had to do a few practices. Once we arrived in Marseilles, I was told to stay out of sight of people on the dockside as much as possible. The next day, the owner and his guests came aboard with crates of supplies, and we were off to sail round the Mediterranean for a few weeks.

By this time, I loved life onboard, and sailing round the islands was a great experience. When we landed back in Marseilles, I was transhipped to another vessel late one night.

We set sail to go back to England, another boat for repair. It was later in the season, so the return trip was not so enjoyable as the weather was quite rough at times. Off the Cornish coast the yacht hove to, and someone rowed a boat out from shore. I was lowered over the side along with two crates of nice brandy and rowed to shore. I was left in no doubt that the crates of brandy were the most important cargo. One of the rowers took me home with him, and I dossed down in front of the fire in his cottage. His wife found me some clean clothes, and I was able to have a thorough wash after weeks of washing in sea water. Then it was into a van and off to the railway to join a train for London with my rail ticket and a ten-pound note!

Uncle Wilfred met me at Paddington Station and took me home with him. I asked a few questions, trying to find out what had happened to the other members of the group, but he told me it was all sorted out and I had to move forward.

Much later in life I tried to find out what happened to the rest of the gang, but to no avail. I tried archived copies of the local paper when I became computer literate but still had no luck.

Reflecting on this episode, I still have no idea why it was necessary to disappear so completely and in such a way as to put me in mortal danger. No one really asked any questions as to what it had been like or how I felt about the situation. I guess I was very fortunate to be overweight with no obvious curves, straight hair, glasses, and a sense of adventure.

Much later in my life with access to the internet, I trawled through old local newspapers, but I could not find any reports that related to a court case about a group which, on reflection, could have been considered a terrorist school. As for no-name boys, well, they were all town boys. I didn't know any town children apart from the girls who attended my high school, and the boys only ever referred to each other by their numbers.

A PASSPORT TO THE WORLD

THE NEXT DAY, Aunt Ethel took me to get a decent haircut, and then to a department store to buy me sensible underwear, shoes, winter coat and other clothes.

We spent that evening sewing name tags into everything because the next day Aunt Ethel and Uncle Wilfred took me to Hillingdon Hospital. This was in early November, and I would be eighteen in late December and able to start my nurse training the following January. I was going to be employed as a nursing cadet in the intervening weeks.

There were two other cadets, both Irish and placed there to keep them out of mischief—like me! Considering they were convent school educated they knew far more than I did about men, so they continued my education in that sphere.

We lived on the ground floor of the nurses' home and were sent to work in a variety of places, behind the scenes as it were. I spent time in the sewing room where sheets and pillowcases were repaired, uniforms altered and the ladies indulged in gossip, most of which went over my head completely, but some that I recognised as being rather scurrilous.

I was fascinated by the large machinery in the laundry, especially the rollers for ironing the sheets. Having grown up using mangles and then ironing sheets by hand, this was a revelation. We sometimes delivered parcels to the wards, which was useful for teaching us the geography of the place and which of the ward sisters were dragons.

I worked with the housekeeper for a while, and she had a typewriter in her office that I was allowed to play on when she was at meetings, so I made the most of that and typed my letters home.

Then it was three years of hard work and study. We all persevered because a British registered nurse certificate was our passport to the world, and we knew we need never be out of work with that in our pocket.

We spent the first three months in the preliminary training school. During the last month of this time, we were sent to work on the wards for four Saturday mornings to break us in gently as it were.

My first morning on the ward was much more than I expected. After the night/day handover, the staff nurse took me aside and said I would have to help her. She was not happy about it, but there was a job to be done! With that, she took me to lay up the trolley for performing the last offices. She pulled the screens round the first bed in the ward, and we began the ritual of laying out the body of a male patient who had died at the handover time.

Apart from Robert, this was the first time I had ever seen a dead body, but a completely nude male was something else again. However, the staff nurse was very matter of fact about the whole process, and I did my part in assisting and survived to tell the tale. We had to report our experiences to our tutors the following Monday. One of them was rather horrified, but Miss Nuttall was of sterner stuff and commented that laying out bodies was part of our task so whether we encountered it early or late was of little consequence.

Our formal education took place during six-week blocks of study without work on the wards. The rest of the time we worked split shifts six days a week except on the day before our rostered day off, which was an 8 am to 4 pm shift. In those days, visits to other organisations were few and far between, but I remember a couple of them very well.

One such visit was to a sewerage farm. I can't remember its official title, but we were duly instructed on the passage of waste through the system. At the end of the tour, we were offered morning tea in the shape of rather fancy biscuits and glasses of sparkling water. After we had indulged in these luxuries, we were informed that the water we had drunk was one of the end products of their labours.

Another visit was to a museum of health and hygiene where we were led through the development of the flushing toilet, together with an insight into laboratory processes for identifying bacteria using agar plates.

We all washed our hands thoroughly, then we were shown how to take scrapings from underneath our fingernails, plate them and hand them over for processing. About a week later, one of our tutors handed us each a piece of paper with the results of our own scrapings. Up until then I had tended to bite my nails rather than file them. I was horrified at my results, but it proved a marvellous incentive to give up the practice of putting my fingers in my mouth.

Soon after we had completed our first school session and began work on the wards, one of the staff nurses became very friendly. This was sort of nice, but I couldn't work out why I felt uneasy about it. This uneasy feeling grew, but I didn't have anyone I could discuss the situation with. I had never heard the word 'lesbian' or anything at all in relation to female relationships.

Growing up in the villages, I had gathered that sometimes men did mysterious things with other men. Everyone avoided them as much as possible, but it was something I did not have a name for, and I had no idea that there were female counterparts. As a lowly student nurse, it was not possible to fend her off. With no inkling of how to explain it and no idea who I could complain to, I was totally confused.

I developed laryngitis during the winter toward the end of my first year, but there was no chance of a couple of days in the warm and resting my voice which had been the treatment when I suffered it as a child, so it took a while to resolve. My voice did not return even though my larynx was perfectly fine.

With hindsight, I can recognise this as my cry for help. I was examined by ENT specialists and other doctors of note over the next few months, all to no avail, and I continued to whisper my way through life.

After nearly twelve months of this, someone arranged for me to see a visiting psychiatrist. After a long chat, seemingly about nothing, he asked me if I knew how to get to Ealing Broadway, which was one suburb away on the number 25 bus. He gave me an address and told me to be there at 3:00 pm sharp the following Tuesday. You didn't argue with a doctor, so I did as directed.

The address appeared to be a normal house in a residential street. I knocked on the door and was somewhat surprised when it was opened by a nun in full habit. She welcomed me, asked me to follow her down a corridor and opened the door into their chapel.

There were other nuns in there, and my escort gave me a psalter opened at the right psalm and explained it was choir practice and asked me to join in whenever I felt like it. I was speechless with surprise, but I sat down and became lost in the music. They sang

Gregorian chant beautifully. After practice I was invited to stay for afternoon tea.

I returned there on Tuesday afternoons for three months, and by the third week I was joining in and loving it. I was also able to talk to one of the older nuns in a way I had been unable to before. She was a great help and gave me great advice for handling relationship matters.

Becoming involved with a psychiatrist also caused the senior staff member to withdraw her attention, and I no longer had that underlying worry. All of this gave me a way to regain my voice without loss of face or other explanations.

Our working conditions as student nurses were so different to the present day, and there are aspects of it that I almost shudder to remember.

The hospital had three geriatric wards. The patients came in with various illnesses and were given the best medications of the day, but so many of them never improved enough to even consider returning home and the wards became their home. They were long wards with beds ranging on both sides, one bathroom and two toilets.

The British took a long time to even consider the shower instead of the bath. Each ward had a bed bath book where we recorded which patients had been bed bathed each day; they usually got one bath per week.

There were no facilities for them to sit comfortably, so they spent all day in bed and bed sores were common.

The sisters in charge of these wards were older women at the end of their careers, and I used to wonder what it must be like to work in that situation knowing it was likely where you were going to end your days. Most of them would have spent their working lives living in nurses' homes, and when they eventually retired, they usually gravitated to small hotels or boarding houses.

Annexe 8 was the gynaecological ward, and there were always several girls who had suffered back-room abortions, become infected and needed surgical attention. They were treated with the utmost distain by the sister in charge.

She had no pity for their situation and never attempted to understand their plight. The rest of the staff on the ward did our best to help these girls, but we trod a fine line.

The men's medical ward was another area we student nurses dreaded. When I think back to some of the treatments of those days, I realise it was little short of a miracle that so many patients were able to go home.

Patients admitted suffering from a variety of cardiac conditions were prescribed complete bed rest for up to six weeks.

By today's standards it was the worst treatment possible, as modern treatments include regular exercise to prevent deep vein thrombosis and a diet that includes actual food. These poor patients were given 30 mL of water per hour, later increased to include milk. First meals were usually mashed potatoes served with tripe in white sauce, or boiled fish.

The sister in charge was a great tennis player but a hard taskmaster at work. I remember one stint on night duty during my third year on that ward.

During one night we had four deaths to deal with. Each of these involved a fair bit of paperwork, plus the ritual laying out of bodies before transfer to the mortuary. All very time consuming and added to the already high workload of the rest of the ward.

When the day staff arrived, I had not completed my written report and there was still one body to be laid out. It all had to be completed before I was allowed to leave the ward—two hours late.

Years later, when I heard that Sister M had suffered a stroke on the tennis court, I found it hard to muster any charitable thoughts.

Regarding our night duty as students, during our first year we were the runners. That meant that each night we would be assigned to two or three wards to help the nurse in charge of the ward with the heavy task of settling the patients.

After the third ward it would be time for our meal break, then back to each ward to relieve the nurse for her break, then start the round again for the early morning routines on each ward. We went off duty exhausted.

During our second-year night duty, we were left in charge of some wards, with regular visits during the night from one or other of the sisters on night duty. By the third year we were deemed able to cope with any ward with our own supply of first year runners.

By modern standards, leaving unsupervised student nurses in charge of hospital wards sounds rather dreadful, but this was during the late 1950s when treatments were much less sophisticated.

For example, an intravenous infusion was relatively rare, and a blood transfusion was very seldom seen. They were all administered through red rubber tubing that had to be super cleaned before being sent to be resterilised. We also had the company of female orderlies for part of each night.

Like the nurse runners, they usually ran between wards. They washed the crockery after the evening tea round, set up the trollies for breakfast the next day, and helped the nurse during the night filling the drums with cotton wool balls and dressings which were then taken to be sterilised for dressing rounds the next day. Most of them were older women who often dispensed good advice and supplied a shoulder to cry on at times.

They also proved their worth at times when unexpected dramas began to unfold in a ward. They all knew how to call the telephone switchboard operator and get him to find the night sister and notify her of the problem while the nurse on duty dealt with the patients.

I think most of us enjoyed the time we spent on the TB wards. In those days the patients seemed to be either young or old, with no middle-aged patients. The ward had French doors down both sides, and these were kept open year-round to allow for fresh air circulation.

During the freezing winter, the patients were buried under mounds of blankets and they each had two hot water bottles. As student nurses we did 'bottle rounds,' collecting one hot water bottle from each patient, refilling them in the sluice room from the steriliser and then wheeling them back to the ward. What would occupational health and safety make of that!

When it came to ward cleaning, the sister in charge made it into a fun day!

Beds from one side of the ward would be pushed over between the beds on the other side, then the cleared side would be swept with very large brooms. Following this, sloppy polish would be thrown onto the floor and the polishers would go into action. These were large bricks covered with old towels or other soft materials and attached to the end of long poles.

The bricks were on a hinge, and we swung them to and fro across the floor to spread the polish and buff it to shine. All the staff participated, and the sister played cheerful records on her turntable! Then the whole thing repeated on the other side of the ward before it was time for a well-earned lunch.

Even in those days this hospital was known for its international mix. My Preliminary Training School (PTS) group had three English girls, one Irish, two Chinese, one Nigerian, two South African and one French.

An odd mix, but we stuck together and shared our joys and sorrows, often in the bathroom on our floor, sitting on a board across the bath with our tired feet soaking in soapy water. Sometimes smaller celebrations were held in individual rooms, and depending on the occasion we might all congregate with our little medicine glasses and share in a bottle of Advocat or Cherry Brandy, both the sort of 'in' drinks of the day. Baby Cham and Star Wine came later.

Beryl, the Nigerian lass, scored a Saturday off, which was almost unheard of for PTS girls, so when she returned, we all wanted to know how she had spent it.

She calmly announced that she had got married! Her husband was a law student at Oxford and a weekend off was a good opportunity. She continued to live-in until the end of our training.

The French lass was also romantically engaged with an American serviceman and, unfortunately for her, she fell pregnant. However, the sisterhood rallied, we all kept quiet and supported her, and on graduation night, she collected her certificate with great aplomb in a uniform twice her normal size so that her pregnant shape was suitably disguised.

I'm sure administration knew of her condition, but I think they knew her father and that swayed their behaviour.

The attention of the staff nurse during my first year and her wish for our association to be secret made it difficult for me to establish much in the way of friendships with the rest of the group. However, once I began attending the nuns' choir practices and began using my voice again, I made friends with Terry, and we have maintained that friendship over the years.

When she and John got married, I was invited to the wedding.

It was held in a church in the city of London, which was a very popular venue. I arrived a bit early and found myself in a large crowd of people, none of whom I recognised, but I presumed they were family friends or relations. It wasn't until the new bride and groom came down the aisle that I realised I was at the wrong ceremony.

Apparently, the whole schedule was running behind time, so Terry and all her guests and family had to circle the block until the previous wedding party left. Her wedding day was a rather long day out for me as the reception was held quite a distance away and it was well after midnight before I got back to the nurses' home.

I was on my final stint of night duty when my twenty-first birthday rolled along and, like those before, it passed with no special celebrations. When I went back to the village for a couple of weeks before I began my midwifery training, Connie and Bob asked me what I would like as a belated present.

In those days it was the usual thing to either give a wristwatch or a string of pearls. I already had a watch, and I certainly didn't belong to the twinset and pearls brigade, so I asked for a record player. I know they didn't think it an appropriate gift for such an occasion, but they bought one anyway. The only LP I had for quite a while was Moura Lympany playing Greig's Piano Concerto. I still enjoy that music.

My father also sent a present for Connie to give to me. It was a single premium bond worth one pound. Apparently all three of his children were thus endowed, as he said, 'With the chance to win thousands.' The bonds were like lottery tickets with numbers being drawn once a month.

MIDWIFERY

ONCE I WAS QUALIFIED AS A STATE REGISTERED NURSE, I applied to a midwifery school. Graduates were expected to stay at their training hospital, where post-graduate short courses were often offered as an incentive. However, I began my midwifery training at Plymouth Freedom Fields Hospital almost immediately mainly because I didn't want to wait a further six months before the next intake of pupils. The midwifery unit at Plymouth was considered the best in the southwest and catered to a vast number of the unusual or abnormal cases in the area.

This meant that while we were being taught the basics of normal midwifery, we were also working in a specialist unit for eclampsia and many more anomalies in midwifery.

One small wing of one ward was specially equipped for eclamptic patients, with two rooms were kept darkened, with very quiet surrounds, all designed to create the least disturbance, while treatments with icy cold enemas were given. Nowadays, I think better antenatal care allows for treatment of the raised blood pressure before it reaches the critical stage. We also delivered babes expected to need partial blood exchanges due to Rhesus incompatibility.

These exchanges were usually carried out in an unused nursery through the umbilical cord. The babe was usually sedated with a brandy-infused bottle of warm boiled water.

Being sent out on a flying squad for emergencies that were not able to reach the hospital in time was another variation. In fact, my flying squad experiences came after I had qualified.

It was a poor offering by today's standards. The aid offered comprised an ambulance driver with a driving licence (not necessarily any other qualification) and a trained midwife. A typical scenario was a call-out to a tenement building, possibly third floor.

With no lifts and possibly no running water except one tap to each floor. There was a family to each room, and sometimes there was one toilet on the floor. While it seemed exciting when I was first sent out on these jobs, I learnt to dread the callouts.

It was very hard work, especially if we had to chair the patient down all those stairs. While we all knew of the poverty in the town, it was difficult to come to terms with it when comparing it to our lives.

There were two specialist obstetricians in attendance, one strictly Catholic and the other with a more liberal view of the world. Mr C was a rather small man who drove a rather large Daimler car.

When he drove by, one only saw his homburg hat and gloved hands on the wheel. If one of his patients was unfortunate enough to be delivered of a severely malformed child that was very unlikely to survive, such as an anencephalic babe (one with no discernible head), he would insist it be bathed and dressed and brought to the mother and insist she breast feed. As you can imagine, this caused a great deal of stress to staff and the mother too. Then he would insist that she attempt to continue to breast feed.

Mr D, however, had a much more liberal approach. Badly deformed infants were wrapped after delivery and wheeled into the sluice room. The cot was left under an open window until the labour delivery was completed, then he would examine the child and determine its future care.

He never insisted on it being held and fed by its mother. These differing approaches presented ethical and moral dilemmas for many of us, and although we discussed it between ourselves, there was nothing in the way of counselling or explanations in those times.

One day, the sister in charge was racing around asking each person what their blood group was. I had no idea why, but when I said that mine was A positive, she grabbed me by the arm and raced me into a room where the mum-to-be was lying on a trolley ready to be raced to theatre for an emergency caesarean operation.

She was bleeding heavily from a placenta praevia. I was perched on the end of the trolley while a doctor set up a direct transfusion from me to the patient. We raced down corridors, into a lift, more corridors and finally into an operating theatre. Both the mother and baby survived. I was sent back to the ward and told to have a cup of tea and then get back to work.

The first part of midwifery training was in a hospital setting, then we had to learn how to cope with home deliveries. For this it was usual to be sent to country towns where they had a small maternity home, but also some midwives who delivered babies in their homes.

I went to Bridgewater in Somerset for this. The pupils were based in a small maternity home in the town, but we pupils worked with the midwives who did the home deliveries. Our area covered all the small villages round about. Before I went there, I had purchased a small scooter, a 49cc Daimler Putsch.

I was slightly afraid of it, but it made life a lot easier than pedalling a bicycle. The maternity home was licenced to take four students, but only two of us turned up for my school. This meant that all the bookings were shared between two instead of four.

We tried to go to the cinema on our evenings off several times, but we never managed to see a whole film. The usherette would come and winkle us out to go back to work. This situation also meant we both gained much more experience than usual, and when I applied to return to Freedom Fields in Plymouth, they made me welcome.

I went on several flying squad trips at Plymouth. On one trip we had to cross the Tamar River on the ferry, then to a small village in Cornwall.

Coming back with the labouring mum onboard, the ferry chains broke, and the ferry began drifting up the river. I delivered the baby during all this commotion, and we all eventually got back to the hospital.

Later I was asked if I could remember where the ferry was at the time of birth because they needed to know which parish the child had been born in to enter it on the birth certificate.

I shared a flat with three other girls and was enjoying life. I had discovered boys and began going out with Derek. He was a sub lieutenant, and his main attraction was his excellent ballroom dancing, something we both enjoyed. One day I answered a knock on the door. The lady standing there asked for me by name and introduced herself as Derek's wife!

She had to come in to make the pot of tea to revive me! Apparently, I was not the first extra girlfriend for Derek, so his wife had to inform other lasses of his duplicity. Their family home was in Portsmouth, but the frigate fleet quite often had prolonged stays in Plymouth either for repairs or for naval exercises.

The other girls had not realised just how naïve I was, so they took me in hand and taught me how to sort the sheep from the goats as it were. Advice that has stood me in good stead ever since.

AUSTRALIA AHOY!

SHORTLY AFTER THAT, I went up to London for days off and just happened to walk past Australia House. They had a big notice in the window that said, 'Come to Sunny Australia. Only Ten Pounds!' This is where the term ten-pound pom originated.

How could I resist such an offer? I went in to find out more. The deal was that you stayed and worked for at least two years or else you had to repay the government for your outbound passage. I had to have a chest X-ray and medical examination, and they also supplied plenty of information regarding employment, so I was able to obtain a position as a midwife before I left home.

When I returned to Plymouth and handed in my resignation, one of the South African registrars took me aside. He taught me several procedures that are not usually performed by midwives in the UK, but he thought they may be useful to me if I went bush nursing!

I had no real concept of what bush nursing meant, but I have thanked him several times over in my mind for his thoughtfulness.

Dealing with the family was easier than I had expected. I don't think they understood that Australia was on the other side of the globe and that my ten-pound passage meant I had to stay for at least two years.

Three months later, March 17, 1962, I arrived at the Tilbury docks to board the good ship SS *Arcadia.* It was a wet, cold and a miserable day, so it was great to board this enormous ship to find my allotted cabin on F deck.

It was a six-berth cabin, six single girls travelling out to new lives. Surprisingly, we all got on remarkably well, although I never got to know any of them well at that time. We only seemed to meet when we went to the cabin to sleep or change clothes. Compared to modern travel arrangements, it was primitive with communal ablution blocks on each corridor and laundry facilities on the next deck down.

The journey lasted four weeks, so not exactly speedy, but all the sights and smells and the enormous space of the ocean made time pass very quickly. Also, it was the first long spell of doing nothing that I had ever had.

Our first port of call was Pireas, where many Greek migrant families came aboard. While they were embarking, we had the opportunity to visit Athens on tours.

It was later, during our passage through the Suez Canal, before I really realised what a major step this was in my life. A sobering thought but too late to change my mind, so step forward and get on with it.

The next port was Aden, and we went ashore in tenders to explore the famous markets. We all kept a very tight hold on our bags all the time.

The Royal Navy ship *Ark Royal* was in port at the same time and by chance a group of officers walked onto the wharf as we disembarked from the tender. That is where I had my last meeting with Derek. He had transferred from the frigate fleet. He introduced me to some of the others in his group as a previous dancing partner and we parted as friends.

We then endured a long haul down to Colombo in Ceylon. Another venture into the markets and a ride on a local bus to a beautiful beach. I was escorted by a fellow passenger who had been there before and knew his way around. He was good company apart from occasionally trying to entice me to sample the delights of a session in the lifeboat.

Our first port of call in Australia was Freemantle. Only those disembarking were allowed ashore, and our stay was relatively short, but they did take on some fresh supplies which included fresh milk! I think we were all heartily sick of the dreadful powdered milk used onboard. Little did I know that later in my life I would become accustomed to using Sunshine milk without complaining.

One lass from our cabin disembarked in Freemantle. She had travelled out to join her fiancé and marry him, but she had not met any of his family and worried that she would not like her future mother-in-law. With no easy telephone contact, no Skype, and no internet, it was a different world.

We chugged round to Melbourne where two of us in the cabin disembarked. Until Brenda began sorting out her luggage and I noted her address label, we had no idea that we were both headed for the Royal Hobart Hospital. It felt much less scary now that we at least had each other to talk to and compare notes.

The migrant program was very well organised. We were shepherded through customs and all other procedures, taken out to the airport, and put on the plane to Hobart. The plane was a Fokker Friendship, with all the passengers being migrants from the ship.

It was the first flight ever for just about everyone, so I could almost feel the release of tension when we finally became airborne and could stop worrying about what might be at the end of the runway if we didn't make it. At Hobart Airport, Brenda and I were met by a taxi driver who was assigned to drive us to our accommodation in Newtown, not at the hospital itself.

HOBART HOSPITAL

WE WERE WARMLY WELCOMED, shown our rooms, and then escorted down to the hospital to be allocated our uniforms, meet the lady superintendent and be given our rosters for the following fortnight.

Neither of us had ever had any contact with nursing sisters' veils. It was a large square of white cotton that had to be precisely folded and starched to within an inch of its life and pinned at a pert angle on our heads.

It took a while to really gain the knack, and I'll admit there were some days when I went around with a very floppy creation on my head.

As a British-trained midwife with experience, I was welcomed to the midwifery ward. The sister in charge was not very tall, rather solid in build and referred to behind her back as 'Tubby.' After a few weeks, I was promoted to teach the practicalities of delivery to the pupil midwives.

This was 1962, and the labour suite consisted of several rooms where women in the last stages of labour prior to delivery were nursed.

The labour ward itself was a very large room with a curtain dividing it crosswise. There was a delivery bed on each side of the curtain, so when we were busy with two women about to deliver simultaneously, part of the curtain was pushed back and I could stand in the middle and supervise both sides together, rather like a policeman directing traffic. Modern midwives would shudder at the thought, with the current trend for spa bath deliveries.

I thought I would be reprimanded following the delivery of one of a visiting specialist's patients. Her progress had been a bit slow but in the final stages she certainly put a spurt on.

The specialist was out at a dinner function when we finally reached him. He suggested that we hold it back 'til he arrived. I had been taught that a good midwife never delayed a delivery for anyone's convenience, so I went ahead and delivered the babe plus the third stage. I was in the process of bathing the mother prior to returning her to her room when he finally arrived. I think he must have stayed at dinner for the after-dinner port. He was not amused, but surprisingly nothing more was said on the matter.

When the apple ships were in port loading, we were often invited to parties onboard. At first, I didn't understand our host's requests that we bring large handbags. Premium quality apples were being exported, and sometimes a crate would be broken in the process, so very nice apples would be available to give to their guests.

Going through the dock gates checkout with bags of apples might have appeared suspicious, but no one would ask to look in a girl's handbag.

I had a fake fur full-length coat at the time, and the lining both at the hem and the ends of the sleeves had been sewn to the fur fabric. There were several nights when I had to be assisted into and out of the taxi because I was loaded with fruit round the hem of the coat and down each sleeve.

Brenda already knew how to drive a car and was looking round for one to buy, so I decided to take driving lessons.

In those days, learner drivers were only allowed to have practice drives on the Domain during the week, but they were permitted to drive on the city streets on Sunday mornings. That was a great help as many streets were one way, and it always helped if I had a preview of what was on my left or right as I drove up or down them.

Brenda eventually found a second-hand car to suit, a Morris Minor. The previous owner needed to buy a bigger car to accommodate his musical instruments, as he played in a band. For ages after that, whenever we cleaned the car, we found loose change in all kinds of nooks and crannies.

After six months in Hobart, we were both offered positions at the Royal Women's Hospital in Paddington, NSW.

We travelled over to the mainland on the ferry and began the drive toward Sydney, enjoying our exploration of the Aussie countryside on the way. At one stage we were driving through a veritable forest of gum trees with peeling bark when we came across an animal on the road. We had no idea what it was or whether it was alive or dead.

We ventured out of the car and approached it warily, each armed with a stout stick to fend it off it if was dangerous. We finally got close enough to know that it was very dead but still no idea as to its identity. A furniture removal van came along the road and pulled up beside us. They informed us that the animal was a wombat and not dangerous anyway.

We arrived at the small town of Nhill toward evening and enquired about accommodation at the hotel. They were undergoing renovations but could put us up in a room with a double bed if we liked. Neither of us had any dire disease, so no problem. The renovations meant that we had to use the toilet out the back, not the one upstairs. We had dinner and remembered not to drink too much!

We hit the road again the next day, and as we drove into Cooma, we were amazed to see so many flagpoles, each waving a different flag. We had no knowledge of the Snowy Mountains Scheme until then, so we made the most of the opportunity and went on a tour around the area.

Our next stop of note was driving into Canberra sounding a bit like a traction engine with muffler trouble. We managed to find a garage with a mechanic able to fix it for us. While we waited, we went to look at Parliament House. My main memory of Canberra was the fact that just about every road had a roundabout on it.

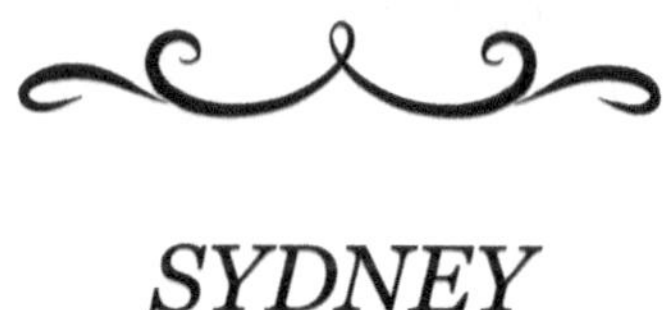

SYDNEY

Fortunately, we drove into Sydney early on a Sunday morning, so navigation to our destination wasn't too much of a problem. The Royal Women's Hospital in Paddington and Crown Street Hospital were the two renowned maternity hospitals of the day. Both have been demolished since.

I was assigned to work in the special care nursery. I hadn't any skills in this area, but I was willing to learn. However, I did not like some of the policies in place.

Naturally, all babes who had endured long or difficult deliveries came to that nursery, together with all the babes destined for adoption. The policy was that all babies were to be cot fed.

My teaching included the concept that touch was an important part of nursery care, and as the adoption babies were often there for at least six weeks, I felt it was quite prolonged sensory deprivation.

I solved the problem by volunteering to do permanent night duty. That pleased a lot of people who were not keen on the night shifts, and the babies had a ball too.

We had a radio, and we played nice music all night, and all the babes got a cuddle while they were being fed. The girls working with me also enjoyed it, so they didn't tell tales!

Brenda and I wanted to get to know the locals, but when we tried to join a variety of clubs, we discovered all of them required we be recommended by an existing member.

I managed to find someone to vouch for me at the All-Nations Club in Paddington, and I was accepted as a member. People seemed to use it mostly for drinking, which didn't interest me, but they did have a camera club, so I joined that. When we had our meetings, I noticed that at the end of the session, all the females would leave the room with the men staying on. When I queried this with another female, she was surprised to realise I didn't know they stayed to view blue movies!

A notice on the board asked for volunteers to show visiting honorary members such as airline staff the sights of Sydney. I volunteered and had a fascinating time, taking mostly KLM pilots on guided tours around the city. I was available from 3 pm 'til 11 pm, then I went home to get ready for a night in the nursery. I was still very naïve, and it was only later that I became more aware of the dangers of being an escort.

But I met some interesting men and often got taken out to dinner.

Brenda and I would go into King's Cross some Saturday nights. We'd both go to the Catholic church—she to confess and me to observe the range of behaviours of the other visitors.

Then we would hail a taxi to go to the Irish Club in the Pyrmont area. Not an Irishman in sight. Nearly all the male patrons were either Italian or Eastern European. No alcohol was allowed, and girls sat on one side of the hall and boys on the other. There was a live band, and every week they highlighted a dance and taught the correct steps.

When the next dance was announced the men would come across and select a girl to dance with. It all sounds very strange as I write this, but we were all there for the dancing. The fact that my partner was often much shorter than me and often had little or no English language really didn't matter. We always had a good time.

Then Brenda found a steady boyfriend, and I decided it was time I explore a bit more of Australia.

At a nursing agency I was offered a position at Narrabri Hospital, so the agency arranged for me to fly there. As I was leaving the office, the lass asked me if I played golf. I replied that I didn't know the first thing about the game, to which she informed me that Daphne, the matron at Narrabri, was a keen golfer!

NARRABRI, NEW SOUTH WALES

DAPHNE MET THE PLANE at Narrabri Airport, and one of her first queries was about my golfing skills. I informed her that I had none but was very keen to learn.

There were two more 'ten-pound poms' working at the hospital—Helen and Maggie—and we soon became firm friends. Daphne arranged for all three of us to have golfing lessons from George, the local stock and station agent who was also a keen golfer.

Part of the golf course was visible from the top floor of the hospital, so when the hospital was not busy, Daphne would occasionally suggest that one or two of us might like to trot over and have a few practice swings. If business looked up, she would get one of the cleaning staff to wave a draw sheet from a particular window, and we would hurry back to work.

The real-life dramas always seemed to happen at night at that place. One night I was on night duty and a rather overweight gentleman died, not unexpectedly. The enrolled nurse and I performed the laying out rituals of the time, and with great effort managed to get him loaded onto the gurney for transport to the morgue. The gurney was the type with one large wheel each side at the middle, two smaller wheels at one end, and just legs at the other. This meant that when wheeling, it was necessary to maintain an even balance.

We managed to get him out the side door and on the unpaved garden path through the orange grove to the morgue. Part way along, the gurney wheels hit a snag, lost balance, and ejected the shrouded body to ground under an orange tree. We were horrified but could see the funny side of the situation, so we laughed hysterically.

We also knew we had no hope of getting the body back on the trolley by ourselves. The hospital was a little way out of town, and the local police were in the habit of cruising over to do a circuit of the parking area at least once during the night just in case we needed help.

As luck would have it, just after losing the body I noticed headlights heading toward the hospital. I raced back to the parking area, waving madly to attract their attention. When I told them we had a body in the orange grove they were very eager.

I didn't mention that it was dead! It was no easy feat, even with two burly policemen, to get the body back onto the gurney. They also undertook to wheel him the rest of the way to the morgue. We left him there on the gurney and hoped we would not require it again during our shift.

Another drama occurred when the local ambulance arrived and unloaded what appeared to be a very singed blanket. They used their sheet to pull it onto the bed we had prepared.

The hospital did not have an emergency section, so emergencies like this went straight to the ward. The ambulance guys explained that it was a young aboriginal girl who had wrapped herself in a blanket to sleep by the campfire but had somehow rolled right into the fire. We started to unwrap the bundle, then we realised that someone had wrapped a second blanket around the lass.

As we delved further and finally reached the patient, we saw that large chunks of skin were going to tear loose if we kept going. As usual, there was only one doctor in town, and he was assisting in this manoeuvre. After we had exposed her head, shoulders, and part of one arm, he called a halt and asked me to get two ampoules of morphia from the drug cupboard and bring them with a 5 mL syringe.

We found a vein on the arm we could see, and he slowly injected the contents of both ampoules. I think we all realised that this was likely to be a lethal dose, but in the circumstances the kindest solution. She would have suffered more if we had put her back in the ambulance to be driven to Tamworth, the nearest regional hospital. She probably would not have survived a complete unwrapping with so much skin debridement.

The doctor then set about re-wrapping the body and we completed it by wrapping the whole bundle in the bed sheet. The ambulance men took on the task of taking it to the morgue. I guess the coroner was informed, and whoever dealt with such events had to deal with the body.

Another night-time drama occurred when a woman who had laboured to deliver her baby for more than twelve hours with very slow progress began to lose strength, with the babe's heartbeat rising rapidly at the same time.

In a modern maternity setting, a caesarean section would solve the problem, but in 1963 in a country hospital with only one doctor available we had to do the best we could. The doctor decided to apply Neville Barnes forceps to retrieve the baby.

These were large scoop-like instruments placed each side of the skull. The doctor often had to apply considerable force to bring the babe down the birth canal. Ideally, there should have been an anaesthetist to administer an anaesthetic.

No such luxury here, so I gave an open ether anaesthetic using a thick wad of combine dressing over the mother's nose and mouth and dropping ether drop by drop onto it until she was sufficiently relaxed to allow the doctor to do what was necessary. Ether is a volatile substance, and I had to breathe off to the side, so I did not also doze off. Both mother and baby survived our ministrations, and I mentally thanked the midwifery registrar who had taught me the basics of such events before I left UK.

Apart from giving us golfing lessons, George was more than happy for company on some of his trips out to stations either picking up wool bales or taking out drums of fuel. Sometimes all three of us would go, squashed into the cab, and George was happy for us to take turns at driving too.

Nowadays I shudder to think of how we approached cattle grids and jump-ups at what I would consider breakneck speeds, but we never came to grief. George was a member of a Returned Services League (RSL) club in Barraba, and if we stopped there on the way home, he would give each of us five pounds with instructions to play the pokies there and lose the lot— George's way of contributing to the club. Sometimes this was hard work as we kept on winning coins back!

We got to see quite a bit of the countryside, and George found a car in a barn on one station which Maggie bought. He transported it back to town to be checked over and registered. Helen did her driving test in it, with me sitting in the back.

It was difficult to keep the car in second gear, so it was my job to start talking to the policeman while Helen shifted up to third gear very smartly. She passed with flying colours.

After the expected six months there I started looking around to see where I might visit next. Queensland beckoned, and I secured a position at Mackay Base Hospital.

MACKAY, QUEENSLAND

MACKAY BASE HOSPITAL WAS OUT OF TOWN, surrounded by cane fields. The taxi from the station dropped me at the entrance to the sisters' quarters.

This opened into the main lounge area where several girls were sitting and chatting. One of them took me upstairs to find my room and give me a general idea of the layout. On the way up the stairs, I was more than a little surprised at the number of frogs all over the place, plus several cane toads.

This was the first time I had seen them, and I was ignorant of their advent and the rest of their story. In the bathroom and toilet area, it was a case of look out for green frogs.

Check under the seat of the toilet before you sat, or you might get a tickle; check the rail of the shower curtain too as one might jump down on you. In the kitchen, always check the inside of the electric jug before you switched on or you may get boiled frog!

Our rooms were rather small, just room for a single bed and tiny bedside table with wardrobe built in. We slept under mosquito nets, and the window area was slatted doors that opened onto a miniscule veranda.

The wall and door onto the corridor were constructed of wooden louvres, which meant that ambient noise floated both into and out of the rooms, but it did help with ventilation.

My introduction to the hospital itself was pretty mind-boggling to say the least.

I was taken over to my assigned ward to begin work on an afternoon shift. It was a thirty-two-bed male ward. Apparently, the morning staff had only begun to work on that ward that morning, so they could not tell me very much about the patients. Besides, they were all going to a celebration that evening so were anxious to get off on time. Nurse Smith and I were left to find our way together.

None of the beds had the patient's name over it, and no one wore an identity bracelet in those days.

I had barely got the measure of the papers on the sister's desk when I became aware of two men in white coats standing in front of the desk. They announced they had come to do their round! I had to ask their names, and it was obvious they thought everyone knew who they were.

They moved to stand at the foot of the first bed in the ward, and one of them held out his hand for the patient notes.

I had to ask the patient his name and then scrabble to find the correct folder. It didn't help that the patient was rather deaf.

Thank heaven for Nurse Smith. She obviously knew this pair, and she leapt to my assistance by pushing the patient folder trolley and handing the correct folders to me. This was after she had done a quick foray forward to ask patients their names.

Not a very auspicious start on my part, and life didn't get much easier. When I was relieved by the night staff it was pouring with rain, so I took a short cut across a lawn area to get back to the quarters.

I had stepped on a few squashy bits during this and presumed it was either toads or frogs. There were several staff in the open lounge area at the front of the quarters drinking tea. One of them commented on my drowned rat status, and I mentioned I had taken a short cut over the lawn area. They replied that I must be brave! It seemed that taipan snakes often lurked in the grass there, and people always came back via the path without stepping on cracks.

I had a much closer encounter with a taipan after that. Early shift on the wards began at 6 am, so someone on night duty was detailed to come over to the quarters to wake those rostered for early shift around 5 am. This meant a knock on the door and a mug of tea and slice of toast balanced on top being left outside the door.

As the rooms were so small and airless, I kept my balcony doors open and slept on top of the bed minus night clothes and under the mosquito net.

As I woke one morning, I realised there was something laying across my legs. I managed to look down without moving my legs to find there was a snake there. I lay back to consider my options and decided that no action was the best!

About half an hour later, someone hammered on my door to tell me I was late for work. I called out, but she didn't wait to hear what I said. Another endless wait before someone else banged on my door. This time she did listen, went away, and came back with someone else and the pass key. She opened my door very gently, peered round it to view the situation, swore profusely and shut the door.

After that, several people peered round the door. By this time, I was past feeling embarrassed at my nakedness, but I was getting desperate to go to the toilet. Eventually, two of the Italian gardeners were brought up to my room to assess the situation.

They peered in at me and had quite a heated discussion. Eventually, they crept into my room armed with garden tools. One of them very quietly untucked the netting and they crouched there, poised for the 'Off' signal.

The netting was flung back, and the offending snake scooped off my legs onto the floor and dispatched on the spot. After a shower and some tea and toast, I ventured over to the ward where I was told I would have to make up the time lost and work an extra couple of hours.

The real crunch for me came later. The hospital trained student nurses, but also ran a two-year midwifery course to enable enrolled nurses to qualify as midwives. I became friendly with one of these midwifery students. She had a car, so we sometimes went out together.

I discovered she was beginning the second year of her training, so I asked whether she had enjoyed her first delivery. It turned out she hadn't quite witnessed the ten normal deliveries required before performing an actual delivery herself. Apparently, several of the local doctors did not like having witnesses (such as nursing students) at their deliveries, and some medical students always took priority over pupils such as her.

I could not intervene for her but advised her to seek help from the nursing union that she subscribed to. Shortly after this I was summoned to matron's office where she said it wasn't appropriate for me to be friendly with students.

I wasn't quite sure what she was implying, but I was not going to be guided by her in such matters. I handed in my resignation at the end of the week. That had proved to be the final straw on what was turning out to be a bit of a disaster in my trip around

Australia. At my final interview with the matron, she informed me she would be notifying the authorities, and I would not get another hospital appointment in Queensland!

BRISBANE

BACK TO BRISBANE BY TRAIN and a room in Centaur House, a refuge for nurses in transit that was maintained by the nursing union. The private hospital I would have preferred to work in did not have any vacancies just then, so I decided to look around.

One evening, I went into a little café for a meal, and there was a group of three people singing acapella to the diners. They were not really performing well, and during one of their breaks I approached them and made a couple of suggestions. The result was that I joined them for the rest of the evening.

They moved between three cafés during the evenings, and the last one provided us with supper. When they heard I was unemployed, one of the girls suggested I go to work with her at the biscuit factory. Why not?

I spent four weeks putting fancy biscuits into their right slots as the tins came along on the conveyor belt. But four weeks was quite enough. One of the lads tried to get me to work with him in the pineapple canning factory, but I knew they had a lot of Māori workers there—rather hot-headed chaps with sharp knives at hand—so I declined his offer and went to work at the repatriation hospital for a few months.

The accommodation for trained staff was in the Valley, a suburb just out from the city, and we were taxied to and from work each day. To get to know the locals, I went to church as advised by my mentors so long ago in Plymouth. That was where I met Clarry, a seminary student learning how to become a reverend gentleman. Over coffee after the service, we discovered we were both keen on dancing, so we began going dancing up in Cloudland, the large dance venue in the city.

Prior to his studies, Clarry had been a window dresser at a David Jones shop in Sydney. Quite a contrast, but I never asked why he had made such a radical change.

The seminary students were required to discipline themselves and not speak to anyone after 6:00 pm on Saturday until after they had taken their first communion on Sunday morning. It was amazing how much we could communicate without uttering a single word!

Clarry decided to take me home to meet his mother. And what a mother! I don't think she had ever called him Clarry, even when he was a baby. It was 'My Clarence' this and 'My Clarence' that. She had very high expectations of him. He was going to be a bishop before he was forty years old if she had any say in it.

I could see her eyeing me off and thinking I wasn't the right sort for holding vicarage tea parties. Meanwhile, I was eyeing her off and thinking she wasn't my idea of any mother-in-law I would ever want. Poor Clarry had to be gently dropped, but I did find him a new girlfriend on the way.

NARROGIN, WESTERN AUSTRALIA

MAGGIE AND HELEN, THE TWO GIRLS I had met in Narrabri, wrote to me to let me know of a position in Narrogin in Western Australia where they were working.

I took the train across to Perth and a bus down to Narrogin. It was good to meet up with them again, and we also became firm friends with Jenny.

Her family lived in Perth, and if Jenny and I had days off together, I would often go home with her. My space in her home was the sleepout on the front veranda. It was a delight to lay in bed at night and hear the surf down on the beach.

Jenny's sister, Deb, had just finished university and had a flat near to her work at the ABC offices. She was a kind of a roving country reporter.

After a while, I was 'adopted' as the third daughter of the house, and Jenny and I developed a sister relationship I'd never had with my blood sisters.

I was envious of the easy relationship Jenny and Deb had with their parents, and I was amazed when their parents included me.

I really appreciated the warmth they extended, and I mourned for both when they died much later, which was something I could not do for any of my family.

Apart from the work, which was typical of small country town hospitals, I was fascinated by the trotting races that were held down there. I had never seen or heard of them before.

Eventually, I met Bruce, whose father trained trotters. He told me a little of how the training was done, so sometimes on my days off, I would go out to the stables and help with the horses. I also learnt quite a bit about trotting, such as how to ride behind a trotter in a spider. I even went into a ladies' race. I came last, but I didn't mind. At least I didn't fall out of the spider.

I quite often got invited to stay for tea in the evening, and I would join Bruce's mother to help with the washing up. She would romanticise about the grandchildren Bruce, and I were going to give them—she even had names picked out—so alarm bells began to clang in my head. I had visions of a shotgun wedding, with me at the end of the gun, so it was time to move on.

I applied for a position as a registered nurse in Darwin. The Commonwealth government paid fares to the Territory and back provided you stayed for a year's contract. I had to attend an interview in Perth and undergo a medical examination, and then the journey to Darwin was booked and I flew there on the mail plane.

DARWIN, NORTHERN TERRITORY

IN MARCH 1965, I began a new chapter in my life. The flight to Darwin left Perth late at night, and we landed at all the little towns on the way to deliver and collect mail. I arrived in Darwin around 6:00 am. The taxi driver was Greek with non-existent English skills and an overpowering aroma of garlic about him, but he knew to drop me off outside the sisters' quarters on Lambell Terrace.

There was no one in sight, but I could hear voices, so I went down the corridor and arrived at the staff kitchen.

It seemed that all the people working there that day were Italian or Greek, again with very little English, but one of the women sized up the situation and took me upstairs where we walked along the corridor until I found a room with my name on the door. The key was in the lock, so I went in. I was tired after my night of flying, so I lay on the bed and slept.

I was woken about eleven o'clock by the home sister saying, 'Come along, I am taking you to see Matron.' She took me over to see Miss Downer, who said, 'How nice to see you. Now I hope you haven't unpacked because I am sending you to Katherine for a few weeks.' At this stage, I didn't know if Katherine was a place or a person, but I thought, *it can't be worse than Mackay.*

I duly arrived in Katherine and went on a very steep learning curve. I was put to work on the ward for Aboriginal patients—a real shock to the system. I had nursed Aboriginal patients in Narrabri in NSW, and Narrogin in WA, but they were all much more sophisticated than the ones I met in Katherine.

The outside walls of the ward had metal louvres which did not quite go down to the ground, but at least ward cleaning was an absolute whizz. All you did was put everything up on the beds, give the room a good old hose down and you were done.

I had patients, boarders, and camp people to look after. In those days no one wore a wristband, so working out 'who was who' took me a little while until I started to recognise faces.

When it came to medications, everybody got vitamins; that was a great help. But the actual medications sometimes went astray because it took me a while to work out how to phrase the questions, so I got what approximated the truth as opposed to what they thought I wanted to hear. They were trying to be obliging, more than avoiding their medication, although avoidance was on the cards for some if the medicine tasted foul.

All patients and boarders were allocated a bed or a cot, but when it came to settling down for the night, that was not necessarily where they were. All the mattresses ended up on the floor. There would be a tangled heap of bodies. Kids all slept with their mothers anyway, so before I left for the night, I did a headcount.

That ward was not staffed during the night, but anybody who was sick was taken up to the main hospital ward which was air-conditioned and housed the white patients and the maternity ward.

Once I settled into the routine, I began to enjoy the experience, but life had its ups and downs. One day I decided to give the sluice room a good going over. In those days we sterilised everything by boiling, so we had two big sterilisers in this room. I threw everything possible in, including half a dozen heavy-duty plastic bed pans. When I pulled them out they resembled way-out art forms? My heart sank as I imagined I would have to pay for them to be replaced. I took a couple up to Sister O'Keefe—she was in charge that day—to ask her advice.

'Mmmmm! How many times have you given one of these out?' she asked.

I replied that I never had.

She said, 'Bring the rest up here; they will look good in my garden.'

Nothing else was ever said about it and later, when I knew her better, I used to visit her home and the pans were there amongst the plants.

The linen cupboard was always kept locked. One day I put the clean linen away in the morning and thought no more about it.

After lunch everyone went outside, which was a bit unusual, but it gave me time to finish some paperwork. Later in the afternoon I went to the linen cupboard to get some nappies. Not a skerrick in there! Nothing—all the shelves were bare.

It was like a bad dream. I shut the door again, opened it up but still nothing there. Then I noticed a little window high on the wall with a couple of louvres missing, so I went for a walk.

Everyone was gathered under the big trees by the camp, and a big card game was in progress. There were piles of sheets, nappies, nightdresses, and every other thing beside various players, obviously being used as stakes in the game.

I think they were expecting me to make a scene, but I just stood there, which proved to be more unnerving for them. The game gradually halted, and everyone sat there looking at the ground.

'I'd like all of this back in the cupboard before tucker time please or I might have to send the dinner trolley back to the kitchen,' I said.

I turned round, walked off and left them to it. I went up to the main block to see whether I had done the right thing or not. The staff on duty there thought it all very funny.

The linen all came back in dribs and drabs, heavily laced with red dust, but who cared about things like that so long as they got their tucker that night?

Our living quarters were pokey in the extreme. There was just room for a little single bed, a kitchen-type chair beside it and a rickety cupboard with a sliding door as a wardrobe. The rooms were not big enough to take an overhead fan, so we had a desk fan balanced on the chair along with a clock. The power went off regularly due to the fruit bats roosting on powerlines (nothing much has changed in relation to the bats!). We had no flywire on the hopper windows, so the mosquitoes had a good feed every night.

At that time, we only had one doctor at the hospital. It was not 'til the next year that a private GP came to town. Sometimes the hospital medico would have to go bush for a day, at a settlement, or a cattle station, and we were left in charge. If anyone required surgery at any time it was a major event.

We had to contact Darwin, then we'd put the patient and escort into the ambulance and off we'd go on the drive up to Hayes Creek where we would meet up with the ambulance that had driven down from Darwin. We'd hand over the patient and return home again.

Timing wasn't always perfect. During the wet season the rivers would be up. We took the Katherine ambulance over the Edith and Ferguson River railway crossings several times when the water was too far over the road. Driving the ambulance onto the track with one wheel inside the lines and the other bouncing over the sleepers with a raging torrent underneath could be a very scary experience. Depending on the day, there was always a chance of meeting up with the train.

By the time I was due to leave Katherine and return to Darwin, I was beginning to enjoy life and getting into the social swing, but I did not have any choice. It was back to Darwin and learning to cope with a different cultural challenge.

In 1965, development in Darwin stopped at Rapid Creek. It was a bush trip to go to Casuarina Beach, and we always took water and supplies such as raisins and sultanas and fruit in case we got stuck.

I was put to work in outpatients-casualty. Many of our patients were either Greek or Italian with very little English. The place would be bursting at the seams in late afternoon and early evenings. While the baby may have been sick all day, Mum had to wait 'til Dad came home from work for transport, and then the school-aged child usually acted as interpreter.

The waiting room was jam-packed one memorable evening when the front door burst open and two men rushed through carrying a third and yelling, 'Snakebite! Snakebite!'

Everybody sat up and took notice. They took the fellow to the treatment rooms in the back, and everyone was wondering what would happen next. Then the door flew open again and another fellow rushed through carrying a big hessian bag, 'I've got the snake! I've got the snake!' It was quite amazing how several patients disappeared, and they didn't come back that day.

AMBULANCE TRIPS

THIS WAS THE TIME just prior to the ambulance service being handed over to the St. John Ambulance service. The hospital ambulances were all old, and the drivers were also the orderlies working around the hospital. No paramedics like the present-day service; the only qualification for the job appeared to be the right sort of driving licence for the vehicles.

I always seemed to be the bunny when someone had to go out in the ambulance. Not that I really minded; it was all an adventure.

But some trips were memorable.

We had gone down the track to pick up a man with a very badly broken leg. When we got back as far as the Elizabeth River, water was over the road and too high to go through. I had nothing in the way of analgesic in the ambulance, so I got out and walked down the line of cars waiting behind us.

'Anybody got an aspirin? You know, aspirin, whatever?'

I ended up giving my patient two Bex powders, and it was all washed down with homemade lemonade donated by somebody in the queue.

When we got back to the hospital, I complained bitterly about the lack of even basic equipment onboard the ambulances and the state of the interiors. I think it was the first long trip I had done. When I arrived for work the next day, I was told to go up and see Dr Dunnett, the medical superintendent—he was God! I thought I was going to be given my marching orders.

However, he asked me about the previous day and then told me I could have the assistance of two orderlies for the day to clean the ambulances to my satisfaction, Also, the matter of the drugs was being dealt with.

The amount of rubbish and dirt we removed from those vehicles was amazing. From then on, we took a drug box, frozen sandwiches, and a water supply on long trips.

Another trip was down to the 42 Mile Peg. That was how we got the messages in those days—it was whatever was the nearest mileage peg. No mobile phones, so by the time we got the message it might have been relayed several times, rather like a game of 'Chinese Whispers" All we were told was, 'There's a bloody mess down at the 42 Mile Peg; you had better go.' So, we went.

When we arrived, there was a truck and trailer off the road and overturned. The driver and his hitchhiker were sitting on the tray playing cards and waiting for someone to help them turn the truck and trailer up the right way. Neither of them needed our services. It turned out the truck had been carting buffalo fillets and that had been the bloody mess. I commented that it was a long way to bring an ambulance and not take anything back on the trolley. The kitchen was delighted with the buffalo meat we took back!

DARWIN SOCIAL LIFE IN THE 1960S

THE HOME SISTER OF THE DAY was Willa Mitchell, an absolute gem. She would let us know when she was going to do an inspection of our quarters, which gave us time to organise the temporary adoption of the assorted wildlife we were keeping. No pets allowed, of course. It was nothing to have half a dozen joeys residing in pillowcases, probably a couple of kittens or cats somewhere, and who knows what else. We used to arrange for the student nurses who lived in the little houses on the campus to care for them during our inspection time, and then we reciprocated when it was their turn.

I always ended up looking after one lass' pythons. They were rather large, but I knew they were not venomous, and she made sure they were not hungry.

In 1965, the banks imported their tellers. They came for a two-year stint, and it looked good on their CV to be able to say, 'I've done two years in Darwin' because from then onwards they were looked at as possible managerial material for a small country town. At the end of each year, half of them would go. Some of them we would weep over, and some we would say 'thank goodness.' Then we would have to wait and see what new talent had arrived for all the social events for the next dry season. It was a wonderful system.

Dry season was ball season, and in those days, there were some balls that you just had to get to. It didn't matter if you went with the biggest chinless wonder in the world.

We went to the balls to dance the night away, and we hardly sat down. There was very little drinking to excess. Entertainment was limited by today's standards, but whatever came to town, we all went.

The Botanical Gardens amphitheatre was the only large venue, and I remember seeing Slim Dusty and his band there. Winifred Atwell came and played her special piano, and the West Australian Ballet Company gave us a bit of culture.

I remember there was great competition amongst those ladies who had room in their houses as to who would provide the billets for the dancers.

When I came back to Darwin after my time in Katherine, I went to church to meet up with the locals. That is where I met Gregory. He worked for the Commonwealth Scientific and Industrial Research Organisation (CSIRO) and was involved in the rice growing project of that time.

He was a keen dancer, too, so we often went to whatever dance was being held. He was my partner for most of the balls. If my days off coincided with his trips out in the bush, he was more than happy to take me along, so I got to see quite a bit of the countryside and learnt quite a lot about the problems of rice growing in an area that had magnificent flocks of magpie geese.

However, Gregory had reached a stage in his life where he was quite keen to get married and settle, so he began to be a bit too amorously intense for me.

I still had a lot of exploring to do and was not ready to settle down just yet. I was at a loss as to how to counter his advances, but I did have a friend who was very keen on Gregory. I put her in the picture, and the next time Gregory had tickets for a ball I phoned him to say I was quite sick. So as not to waste the tickets, I suggested Glenda might be available to go with in my place. My evasion worked well. He and Glenda quite quickly became engaged and married, and I am godmother to their first child, so we are still in touch.

The sisters' quarters had a sitting room on each floor, and amenities included an old treadle sewing machine. There was only one real dress shop in town, and it was a bit pricey for us, so we patronised Doris Mallett's material shop on Cavanagh Street.

If we got the message that she had new stock, we made sure to get there as quickly as possible to be the first one to have our dress made.

There was one shoe shop in town owned by Les Heaven, in Knuckey Street. If he didn't have your size, well, it was too bad, you had to wait for the next ship to arrive and hope there was something on it.

Many supplies were brought to Darwin by ship at that time, mostly up the West Australian coastal route, so if you were eagerly waiting for things to be delivered to the shops you kept an eye on the shipping schedules.

I learnt to water ski, and if there were three skiers available during the dry season, we phoned Roger Rooney, a marine mechanic who worked for VB Perkins.

He owned a good boat and all the equipment needed, and he was often able to meet us at whatever spot he thought was best for the time and the tide. We had some good times with Roger. I shudder to think of some of the spots where we skied now.

I wouldn't put a toe in the water today in some of those locations due to the prevalence of crocodiles, but in those days, they were not a problem. They were still being hunted, so they generally stayed away from human activities.

In the rainy season, we would go down to Knuckey's Lagoon. There was a bush track in from the highway, but you had to keep a sharp lookout for it as it wasn't signposted. There were also a lot of buffalo on the road.

But it was a lovely spot, and there wasn't a bit of habitation for miles around. Now the whole lagoon area is dotted with houses and gardens, and the lagoon has been known to house saltwater crocodiles.

By this time, I had been in Australia for just over four years. I had completed just over a year in Darwin, and my family were beginning to wonder if they would ever see me again, so I booked a passage back to England. Mind you, I bought a return ticket as I knew I could have a much more interesting life in Oz.

RETURN TO ENGLAND

I BOOKED THE SIX-WEEK PASSAGE on the SS *Oriana*. It was my first real holiday for four years. We sailed from Sydney over to Auckland, had a quick glimpse of New Zealand, then we were in for the long haul up to Vancouver.

This time I was in a four-berth cabin with Norma, a middle-aged lady who was good fun, and Charlene, a blonde bombshell type. The fourth berth had been booked by Charlene's business partner, but she broke her leg two days before sailing and was strung up in traction in a hospital bed in Sydney.

Their business was exotic dancing, and Charlene was beside herself as they had bookings to provide entertainment on the trip. She needed an offsider.

She and Norma eyed me up and down and decided I had 'possibilities'!

I didn't have much say in the matter, but I do like a challenge.

I've never been what you might call 'shapely,' so the costume had to have a few nips and tucks put in it.

When on stage, I also had socks tucked into my bra to give me a bit of 'oomph' as it were.

My task as offsider wasn't very onerous, more flitting about and waving scarves and whisking used props off the stage. A few quick rehearsals in the ballroom and opening night was upon us. I was suitably fortified with a stiff gin and tonic, and we were on.

I wore contact lenses at that time, but I worked blind when I was 'entertaining.'

I could see enough to operate, but I couldn't see the audience. It helped, and I've used that tactic in other situations when entertaining. We continued the routine with variations several times on the trip. It was a lot of fun but not something I wanted to take up seriously.

Charlene left the ship in Vancouver, and I wasn't sorry to get off the stage and be myself again.

We cruised down the west coast of America with interesting days ashore, then through the Panama Canal. The trip across the Atlantic was wild, hatches battened, gangways roped, with less than a dozen people appearing in the dining rooms for meals.

I loved it and persuaded a couple of the stewards to allow me to go on deck provided I stay within a certain area and hooked myself onto one of the ropes along the deck.

We arrived in Southampton to find the porters on strike. It was Wembley Cup final day to boot, so my tube journey out to Ruislip, near the end of the Uxbridge line (with Wembley Station on the line), was memorable, especially as I was lumbered with luggage and a very large sombrero.

Uncle Wilfred met me at the station, reviving memories of other times we had met up on train platforms.

After four years in Australia, it was like a time warp to be back in the UK.

My aunt and uncle were delighted to have me back, but they found it difficult to accept the fact that I had seen the world and could not fit back into theirs.

My aunt scoured the neighbourhood for eligible bachelors and manufactured opportunities for me to meet them. She wanted me married off and producing children!

I escaped up to London, ostensibly to spend time with a friend from my nurse-training days, but in truth I went to pay a visit to the All-Nations Club in Earl's Court, locally known as Kangaroo Valley.

I had joined the club before leaving Australia knowing I would find fellow travellers there. I visited their employment office and asked if they could find me a few weeks' work anywhere, so long as accommodation was part of the package. Preferably not nursing. After some consultation, the lass asked me if I knew where Selfridges was in Oxford Street.

'There is a lane along one side. Go down there to a yellow door with 33 on it. Go in and say Susan sent you.'

It crossed my mind that this might be a backdoor into the white slave trade or something, but my curiosity kept me going.

I was greeted with big smiles and a handshake; told they were not quite ready yet and would I like to wait in the room off to the side. This was a very nicely furnished room, comfortable lounges and chairs and a trolley with hot coffee and Kunzle Cakes! These were delicious cakes with cream fillings that were presented in actual chocolate casings—the height of luxury and not to be passed by without tasting. I made myself comfortable.

Shortly after I had settled, the door opened and the receptionist ushered in a well-dressed man who went to the trolley and helped himself, then sat down on the next lounge. The conversation began in typical English fashion, commenting on the weather. Then he asked if I was a visitor to London, and it just flowed from there. After a while he stood and asked me if I would like to go with him into his office!

It was another tastefully furnished room, and he asked me if I had any idea where I was apart from down the lane, etc. I had to admit I had no clues.

'Why, this is the London headquarters of the Billy Butlins empire!' he said.

They ran all-inclusive holiday camps scattered around the coastline of England, Wales and Scotland for workers and their families. They operated mostly in the summer months and were staffed by university students for the lowly jobs and some regular management people.

Apparently, management was causing problems, so this gentleman was recruiting outsiders to work in the camps at run-of-the-mill jobs. We would watch management personnel as directed and report back so the trouble spots could be dealt with.

I was going to be a spy! I was ideal as I was a definite outsider and would be going back to Australia soon.

HOLIDAY WITH A DIFFERENCE

THE RESULT OF THIS CONVERSATION was me boarding the train to Ayr in Scotland.

My job there was to be an assistant in one of the confectionery kiosks. Accommodation was a bit spartan, but clean, and I shared a room with another lass who was studying at Edinburgh University.

She was working in the camp's kitchens, and we hardly ever saw each other apart from going to bed or getting up. Thus, I began my odd job of shop assistant/spy. I was told not to write anything down, just a verbal report. BUT if I was in dire trouble at any time, I was to get myself to the Ayr police station and ask for Mr Jacobs!

A reminder of the times might help modern readers to understand better. This was 1966. There were no mobile phones. The camp had two public phones inside the reception area, so conversations could be overheard. There was one post-box for those postcards home, and I think we needed a good excuse to be allowed to go out and into town, which was a few miles away anyway. As a camper, you had paid for an all-inclusive holiday, so enjoy it!

I went along to watch people at the roller -skating rink each Tuesday afternoon, which was where I was contacted by the person I could report to. Usually, a man would appear beside me and make some comment about one or other of the skaters. His description would give me the clue that I was to spill the beans as it were.

My spying activities were done during my evening shifts in various evening entertainment venues.

I worked as a bar girl, usherette or ice-cream seller. I was to be wherever I might find my target, note who they were with and anything else I thought might be useful.

Not hard at all for a curious soul like me. My targets were changed as I forwarded information, so I did a very comprehensive tour of the camp and all its activities.

One day I overheard a conversation that put my suspicious mind on high alert. I put a few clues together and decided on my moves.

I managed to get myself locked inside the main store depot the following night.

I had no real idea what I was looking for but was having a nose around when I heard a key in the door.

I climbed to the top of a pile of cartons, which gave me a better view of the whole place.

Four men came in, congregated round one group of cartons, and opened one. From my perch, I could see them sampling what looked like a white powder.

Even in those days I knew a bit about the drug trade, and this seemed to fit the bill. I managed to get myself out of there before dawn by picking a lock, a skill I had learnt with the teenage gang all those years ago. I crept back to my room where my roommate was still fast asleep.

My contact was on the following day, so I had to sit on this nugget of news. I was working the afternoon shift in the shop, on the till as usual.

A man I had never noticed before bought a slab of toffee. As I was giving him his change, he said, 'They're on to you. Move!'

I didn't need him to say it twice. I quickly excused myself to go to the toilet, blaming the stew at tea, left the shop and headed down to the stables.

They kept a string of horses and provided horse rides along the sands during the day. As a child I had learnt to ride bareback, with just a bridle, so I managed to get a bridle on one of the horses and took off down the beach to the end of the perimeter wire.

I forgot to mention that the camp was surrounded by high wire fences, presumably to keep out any freeloaders in the local community. The camp had originally been built as a navy training camp and then taken over by the Butlins organization to change into a holiday destination.

Fortunately, it was mid tide, so I only got my lower half wet. Once past the wire, I rode along the sand as far as possible, then we stumbled our way through rough ground until we reached the road. It was dark, and I rode as quickly as possible into town. I found the police station, set the horse free, went in and asked to speak with Mr Jacob please!

Instant action! I was escorted through to the back of the station where I explained as well as I could why I was there.

Several phone calls were made before I was put inside a paddy wagon with many assurances that I wasn't being taken off to jail. After a long trip, we stopped by a rail track. This was where the overnight mail train passed through on its way to London. A train slowed to a crawl as mail bags were tossed out of and into a carriage with the doors rolled back. The guard had obviously been told to expect me, and I was sort of tossed aboard and he caught me before I bowled over. What a way to travel!

The guard shared his tea and sandwiches with me, and we finally rolled into King's Cross Station early in the morning.

From there I was taken by car to a safe house. This turned out to be in Windsor, an area I had cycled round as a student nurse.

I was asked for minute details of a variety of aspects of life in the camp. Then I was asked when I was going back to Australia. I think they sort of hoped it would be soon, but I still had to hang about for Grandma's birthday a few weeks away. A few telephone calls later, I was asked if I would like to spend my spare time in Cornwall. I was quite happy to comply and even happier when they arranged for me to be hotel roustabout at a small private hotel in Mevagissy, a small fishing village with beautiful beaches.

I had a wonderful three weeks filling in either as housemaid, kitchen hand, dog, and children minder and even stints as a barmaid. Life was never dull.

Then it was back to the village and the birthday celebrations. A week after that, I was down in Southampton boarding the SS *Orcades* on the way back to Australia. This time the ship was going the usual route through the Mediterranean and the Suez Canal with a brief stop in Aden to refuel, then Colombo to Freemantle.

I was again in a four-berth cabin. This time my travelling partners were Mrs Smith, a very old lady, and Dell with baby Moses.

Dell was Jewish and had been selected to deliver some important scrolls to a temple in Melbourne.

Moses was a very placid child of five months, so he slept in a cot which had replaced the second lower bunk.

When we arrived at Colombo, I went ashore and the others in the cabin stayed onboard. I enjoyed my day ashore and slept soundly that night.

Dell was in the habit of taking Moses up on deck early in the mornings, so that left myself and Mrs Smith in peace. When I got down from my bunk, I turned to wish Mrs Smith 'Good morning,' but one glance told me she had died during the night.

I went out to find our cabin steward and asked if he could arrange for the body to be removed as quickly as possible. I went on deck to find Dell and put her in the picture so she would stay away from the cabin until it had been cleared.

I knew she would consider herself somewhat compromised, carrying sacred scrolls and the possibility of being contaminated by the events of the night.

I explained this to the purser. We were fortunate in that a Jewish scholar of some note was travelling in first class, so the purser arranged for Dell and me to meet with him to discuss Dell's perceived problem.

He was delighted to meet her and find out about her mission. He assured her she would not be considered unclean.

When we arrived in Melbourne, Mrs Smith's son came aboard briefly to thank those concerned with his mother. It seems she had spent the last few years of her life travelling between the two continents at the expense of her family, so her burial at sea had been a blessing for them.

I got back onboard, and we chugged round to the familiar sight of the opera house sails as we headed for our berth.

Looking back, it had been a very eventful holiday, but I was more than happy to be back in Australia.

Returning to Sydney, I joined Jenny, who was doing private nursing there. She was sharing a flat with two other girls, and they were quite happy to have me camp for a while so long as I did all the cooking.

Jenny and I wanted to explore New Zealand but didn't have enough money to consider travelling right then, so we explored the possibilities of nursing somewhere in Queensland where we could have a warm winter and save hard for our overseas trip. This is how we found an opportunity in Yeppoon, which is on the coast just out from Rockhampton.

YEPPOON, QUEENSLAND

THERE WAS A SMALL COUNTRY HOSPITAL ideally situated right by the beach, and the walk into town was along the beach road shaded by palm trees. Mind you, the hospital, and the equipment in it were quite another thing!

Many of the long-term patients were the elderly of the district with all the ills of old age; some simple surgery was performed, and we also had a small maternity wing with facilities for normal births.

But the equipment was very basic. There was one oxygen cylinder for the whole place, so if one of the elderly patients required it at the same time as a newborn, who made the choice?

Similarly, the supply of syringes was minimal. In those days we used glass syringes, and the plungers tended not to fit the barrels closely as they aged.

Add to this the fact that needles were also in very short supply and were quite often hooked at the ends. These were supplemented by the matron with the needles from the procaine penicillin syringes, which were single-use items with very large bore needles.

Trying to give a very small dose of adrenaline subcutaneously to a wheezing asthmatic patient was very hit or miss. We were never sure just how much of the medication arrived at its destination or how much leaked onto the skin.

Matron oversaw the theatre and administered the pre-operative medication. Nearly all the patients who underwent operations had what we described as 'wet chests' when they returned to the ward. Then one day I happened to be in the right spot to see Matron preparing the pre-op injection.

She was dissolving atropine tablets in sterile water over a little Bunsen burner, a procedure that was practiced in the dark ages. We eventually got the doctor who administered the anaesthetics to insist she get the atropine ampoules that were readily available through the hospital pharmacy system.

Another cost saver for her was the little job she devised for the night staff. All bandages, including gauze, were sent to the laundry to be washed. Night staff would find a bag of tangled crepe and gauze bandages to rewind during the night.

She also cut corners on the intravenous giving sets. These were light plastic meant for single use only. However, we had several asthmatic patients who were given Ventolin infusions to relieve their wheezing.

When the drip was dismantled, the giving set used was to be wrapped in a green theatre towel and placed on the shelf above their bed where it could be rescued and re-used if necessary.

Patient meals were certainly not luxurious and considering that many of the long-term patients were aged and missing teeth, I think they must have spent their nights feeling rather hungry.

Their evening meal consisted of a bowl of vegetable soup with one slice of bread together with a small piece of cold corned silverside, shredded lettuce leaf and carrot.

Staff didn't fare any better. We were served the silverside six nights a week. We also received lettuce and carrot except our salad had a slice of tomato thrown in. Our fruit allocation was usually a slice of unripe pineapple that was only edible if you sprinkled it with salt.

On Fridays, Mrs Higgins, the cook, was given two eggs to prepare scrambled eggs for three staff. Mrs H did her very best with what she was allowed, but there was little in the way of job satisfaction for her.

After a few weeks of this, I took it upon myself to chat with the butcher who supplied the hospital with meat. I commented on the lack of variety and asked if he could supply different things for the same price. He assured me there were plenty of alternatives.

I presented my findings to Ms Moore, who, of course, told me I was meddling in an area that was not my concern. Then I wondered out loud whether the Rockhampton Hospital Board, which also managed Yeppoon, would be interested in my findings, and left her to consider. Mrs Higgins was amazed to find several variations in the provisions arriving a couple of weeks after this, and so were we.

Yeppoon hosted a conchological conference while we were there, so Jenny and I went to a couple of the talks that were open to the public, which fired our interest in the shells to be found on our doorstep. It was illegal to take live shells, but one or two we found were handed over to Mrs Higgins, who buried them in an ants' nest to be cleaned and then returned them to us.

A particular delight was being taken sailing by one of our grateful patients. Spencer had survived a dramatic gastric bleed during his stay in the hospital, and Jenny and I had both 'specialled' him during that time, so he took us sailing round the Keppel Islands.

This was long before they were developed in any way and landing on them was an invitation to millions of sandflies to come and feast. We thought of this when they were being developed as holiday destinations and determined never to go there, but we enjoyed sailing around them. We would throw in a line and catch fish, then cook them on the beach just below the hospital.

We had lived frugally during our six months in Yeppoon, so we felt we had enough saved to explore

New Zealand. We drove back to Sydney to board the SS *Fairstar*, headed for Auckland.

We had to provide a $500 bond before we could take our little VW Beetle with us. This was meant to prevent us selling it while we were over there, as at that time many of the cars in New Zealand were very old and almost tied together with binder twine.

NEW ZEALAND

WE ARRIVED IN AUCKLAND and headed for an employment agency looking for hotel work with accommodation supplied. We were offered posts together as waitresses at the Grand Hotel Rotorua. This was our first foray into this type of work, and the Grand turned out to be a very good place to start.

The dining room was silver service, so Doris, the manageress, took us in hand and taught us the correct way to do it. Rotorua had a sulphurous atmosphere due to all the volcanic activity around.

This affected the silverware, so we sat down to polish every piece twice a week. This was done on Monday and Thursday mornings after breakfast had been cleared.

The hotel catered to a lot of American tourists doing coach tours, and they had their own peculiarities.

At breakfast, their first order was for 'hot coffee.' When it arrived, they would peruse the menu and order food. Hot pancakes with bacon and maple syrup were top of the list. By the time that this arrived, their coffee was cold, so, 'More hot coffee, please.'

At dinnertime, we wore frilly aprons over our dresses and quite often one or other of the women sitting at a table would look us up and down and remark on how cute we looked!

When it came to ordering their meal, the menu always had roast hogget on it. 'What's hogget?' was a regular question. I solved that one by telling them it was teenage lamb. This caused great amusement and increased the consumption of hogget considerably.

The chef was Irish, Paddy by name, and when we went into the kitchen to order he always wanted to know if it was for 'a man, a woman or a horse' I never dared to say it was for a horse, but I was sorely tempted.

'Rare, medium, or well done?'

The meat was always rare, so for a medium request the slice would be dunked into the consommé briefly to cook just a tad more. For well done, Paddy slapped it on top of the bain-marie, then turned it over until it looked right!

The kitchen staff often prepared special salads for dinner, and we would take large bowls round to the tables for the guests to help themselves. One night we had a group of Americans staying over, and one man amongst them requested a table to himself please. It was obvious he did not get along with the rest of the group. This evening, he had been a little late in coming to dinner, so most of the guests were already starting their dessert course when he requested the

Waldorf salad. As I approached his table, I tripped on the carpet and the bowl of salad spilt into his lap!

I was mortified, but Doris leapt into action and helped me clean him off as much as possible. She then assisted him out of the dining room assuring him that the hotel would deal with all the dry cleaning required. I returned from the kitchen with equipment to do a better clean-up job in the dining room to be greeted by a round of discreet applause from those sitting at tables nearby. There were murmurs to the effect that it couldn't have happened to a nicer fellow!

Doris was very thoughtful and gave us days off together almost all the time so we could explore the countryside and experience the delights of the hot pools and other volcanic wonders of the area. Having the car meant we could expand our exploring over to the Bay of Islands and the Coromandel Coast.

We took a trip to the very tip of the North Island. There was a caravan park there, but the owner only had one hut to offer us.

He apologised for its size and let us stay there for one night for free. The hut was little bigger than a hen house, two bunk beds stacked and just enough room beside them to change clothes, but we didn't mind at all.

Overall, the caravan parks throughout the country were very well run with good amenities for car travellers like us.

By the end of three months, we had done all the exploring possible from that base, so we resigned and drove down to Queenstown where we both had jobs as waitresses at O'Connell's Hotel.

This was the most upmarket hotel in the area at that time and was ideally situated on the banks of Lake Wakatipu.

Staff were accommodated in a house about a twenty-minute walk from the hotel, a quick scamper going to work as that trip was all downhill. We ate at the hotel and learnt quite a lot about NZ cheeses and the secret of making superb pavlovas. Several staff left during the month of our arrival, so moving up the pecking order was swift.

Much to my surprise and consternation, I was moved up to be the 'meet and greet' person for the restaurant.

I was on a steep learning curve. In the evenings, I would appear dressed up!

I wore a long shift and full make-up, including false eyelashes. I had long hair that I usually wore in a French pleat, and by a stroke of luck I also had some squiggles—false ringlets and curls attached to combs—to add to this.

After my initial trepidation, I quite enjoyed the job, especially the dinner dances on Friday nights. I had a pair of blue-tinted contact lenses that made my eyes look almost violet. I couldn't see too well with them in, but they were very good for mild flirting, and I'm sure they increased our tips.

The hotel was selected to host the official dinner for a convention of NZ tourist operators being held in town.

Joe, the manager, asked me what I knew about banqueting. Neither of us had much idea, so I went to the local library. After a few telephone calls, the librarian located a book on the topic, but it was down in Dunedin. She arranged for it to be brought over to Queenstown by a butcher who was delivering meat to the town, so Joe and I read it and took notes.

Serving a banquet was in some ways easier than our normal Friday evening dinner dances, and we sailed through it without a hitch.

Jenny and I explored the region on our days off, and as the weather got colder, we gathered fir cones to put on the fire we had in our sitting room. We were also in the house when a large earthquake occurred. Our beds were divan type with drawers under them, so we had no hope of getting under the beds as protection. But apart from things flying around in the kitchen, we suffered no damage. Later, we drove out to Greymouth, and parts of the road going there were quite badly buckled.

We managed to get enough days off together to drive down to Te Anau for the start of the Milford Track walk. This was during the 60s, so the facilities on the way were very basic. We were amazed that all the provisions for the overnight huts where we slept had to be brought there by pack horses.

Despite being rained-in at one hut for a couple of nights, we had a marvellous time, and it was well worth the effort. During our rain-enforced stay in the overnight hut, Jenny, and I both learnt the art of tatting. A fellow traveller was sorting through a bag she was carrying, and we noticed a tatting shuttle and said we would love to learn. In no time at all, she sent her husband outside to find a suitable piece of wood which he then fashioned into what was a very large tatting shuttle. With the aid of some string from the kitchen of the hut, she gave us an impromptu lesson. I still have that shuttle somewhere.

Then winter really arrived snow and ice and bitter winds. Jenny and I were both feeling homesick for Australia, so we arranged a passage for us plus the car on a ship leaving Auckland. We had to get snow chains and fit them to the car to be able to drive out. Because we had not worked in NZ for a whole year, apparently, we owed the tax department money. There were no automatic bank transfers, of course, so we said we'd go to the bank to get the money. We never did, and I must admit I was a bit anxious that tax officers would come and take us off the ship before it left shore.

BACK TO AUSTRALIA

BACK TO SYDNEY and we prepared for the long drive over to Perth. From Sydney to Ceduna was just over 1,000 km, and from Ceduna to Perth was just under 2,000 km. It was a long drive, but we were used to places being far apart in Oz.

We anticipated lots of dust along the Nullarbor Highway, but once we left the bitumen just west of Ceduna, we dropped into a very large puddle of mud, and it was more mud for most of the way.

There were times when we drove on detours round bogged road trains, and sometimes there were detours around detours so we began to wonder if we would ever see the actual highway again.

There were compensations in that the countryside was alive with wild flowers, and animal and bird life. The simple things of life. We were the only guests for the night at one roadhouse, and in the morning, I found myself sitting on the toilet, which was down quite a long path, with the door open and a view of acres of wildflowers and what appeared to be small wallabies feeding.

Back in Perth we were undecided about where we wanted to be or what we would do next, so in the interim we paid for our board with Jenny's parents by repainting quite a bit of the house.

154

INFANT HEALTH

Then we both decided we'd undertake the training for our third nursing certificate in infant health. We had to live-in while doing it, and it proved to be a good way to get back into the nursing world.

The course was taught in a building attached to a children's home in South Perth. There were only six pupils, all of us older than we had been during any of our other stints of training, so we had a wide variety of experiences between us.

But none of us had experience with small children, so we were on a steep learning curve. At times, we were allowed to take small groups of children from the home on outings to parks or places of interest.

This was just before the time when it became obligatory to restrain children in vehicles. The necessity for carrying drinks, flannels to clean faces and hands, and extra pants or nappies taught us appreciation for the lot of young mothers taking their toddlers anywhere.

We were also placed at different infant health clinics during the course so we could witness infant health in practice.

I was sent to the clinic in Bridgewater where I boarded with the infant health sister. She was a very good cook, so we ate very well.

It was also toward the end of the picking season for nectarines in the area, and we were invited to go along and help strip a few trees one evening. I drove back to Perth with several boxes of fruit gleaned from this activity.

Once we had completed the course, Jenny decided to put it to good use and began work as an infant health nurse. Her practice was in the Swan Valley, so she would arrive home with fruit and vegetables that had been given to her by the mothers who visited the clinics.

After a while, Jenny volunteered to work for Save the Children fund in Vietnam, and her parents decided to go back to Malaysia where they had spent most of their early married life, so I was left to house-sit.

By then I had decided to further my nursing education and enrol at Princess Margaret's Hospital for a post-graduate sick children's nursing course.

MARRIAGE

I HAD BEEN GOING OUT WITH PETER for some time, and now we tried out life together. He was French Canadian and working with a firm of architects in Australia. Our relationship progressed to the point where we thought it was time, we became a legal couple. Neither of us had any religious affiliations, so we arranged to be married at Perth Town Hall by the registrar. We followed the ceremony with an up-market pub lunch with Peter's best friend who had been his 'best man' and a few of my nursing colleagues as my support. We didn't need any of the usual fuss, and neither of us had family to consider.

A couple of months later we went to see our GP, who confirmed my pregnancy and noted that Peter had a small sort of pedicle on his wrist.

He offered to remove it, which took about five minutes to perform. But he was a conscientious GP and sent it off to the laboratory. The next week, he came looking for us to say the pedicle had cancerous cells in it and should be investigated.

This was 1969, so there were no scans or ultrasounds then, just X-rays and much poking and prodding.

Just after this, I answered a knock on the door one day to find a young man standing there who was a younger copy of Peter. He asked for Peter, and I said he was at work, but I was his wife, and could I help? He appeared to be shocked at this news, so I invited him in for some water and to find out what was going on.

He was Peter's younger brother sent over from Canada by their mother to bring Peter back to marry his fiancée. Now I needed a drink of water!

Peter had told me he was an only child and that both his parents had been killed in a road accident when he was sixteen. He had been cared for by his uncle, who was dead, so he had no family ties.

As for the fiancée, she was the unlovely daughter of a business associate, and the marriage would help in the amalgamation of the two businesses.

Apparently, Peter's family were considered 'top drawer' people in Quebec and staunch members of the Catholic church. Our marriage would be cause for much gossip and bitter recriminations.

As you can guess, Peter had a lot of explaining to do. I was very confused and hurt by all the deception.

His mother was quite convinced that our civil marriage would not be recognised by the church in Canada, so why didn't he just come home and do the right thing? Our life was thrown into confusion.

I still loved him but found it difficult to understand all the deceit. However, as I got to know his mother, his wish to leave her behind became clear.

I continued with my nursing course. A couple of friends who were also doing the paediatric course did what they could to help me through all this, but they were married with school-aged children and already found the work/home balance difficult.

At least I could talk to them when I needed a listening ear. Peter continued to work between X-rays, blood tests and medical appointments with no clues as to the site of the initial cancerous growth. However, he began to be more and more off colour, lethargic and generally unwell.

He had great difficulty in eating and consequently lost a lot of weight. By the beginning of December his medical team decided he probably had a stomach cancer, and they were also inclined to think that his liver was affected too.

I realised quite early that his illness was going to be terminal, but he refused to consider this outcome and was in denial until the end.

By the end of November, he admitted that going to work was beyond him. I completed my nursing course at the end of November, so I cared for him at home. Peter was admitted to hospital on December 22, and I stayed with him until he died on Christmas Eve.

I telephoned his brother in Canada regarding the situation and left it to his judgement as to whether or when he notified their mother.

I left the hospital around lunchtime on Christmas Day and went home. One of the neighbours gave me a shoulder to cry on and made sure I had a proper meal.

At 10:00 pm I went into premature labour. I had been for an antenatal check a week before Christmas and nothing unusual was noted, but there was no foetal heartbeat right from the beginning of labour. With all the emotional turmoil of Peter's death, I could not remember when I had last felt the baby move. In 1969 there was no thought of rushing off to theatre for caesarean birth, so I laboured on. The midwives caring for me had very little to say, so it was a rather lonely process. I understood. in view of my husband's recent death and the fact that no one wanted their Christmas delivery to be stillborn.

The baby was born at 6:00 pm on Boxing Day, and I left the maternity hospital three days later.

When I arrived home, I found that my neighbours had provided me with fresh food and invited me to join their families for meals.

Peter's best friend Andrew was a tower of strength during all of this and managed to arrange for a double cremation on January 8.

Medical staff had wanted to do post-mortems on both Peter and the baby, but I refused both. There seemed little point in prolonging what was a period of total confusion and loss for me. I needed to move forward.

On the day of the cremations, which were completed by 10:00 am, Andrew asked me what I would really like to do. I did not want to go back to the house for the rest of the day and admitted that a day at sea would be nice.

I felt that wind and waves would be helpful. He took me back to the house to change, then out to Fremantle where we hired a boat, bought some bait, and sailed out over blue water to recuperate from the previous few days.

Late in the afternoon the wind rose, it began to rain, and we were lucky to make it back through the breakwater before the storm arrived. By this time, we were wet, cold, and hungry so we picked up a pizza on the way and headed back to my house for hot showers, dry clothes, and food.

Andrew kept me company during that night, and I was very grateful for that. We kept in touch for several years, until he was killed in a road accident. I think I mourned his loss almost as much as Peter's.

I wrote to Peter's mother to let her know that Peter was no more, and I later mailed his ashes to her.

It was more than ten years before I met my mother-in-law. I was over in the UK visiting with my long-time friend Felicity.

She was quite a socialite and knew all the right people. One day she told me we were going to lunch, and I needed to look my best. I did my hair and make-up, then dressed in borrowed finery from her wardrobe. She told me not to be surprised at anything she might say!

We went to a special lunch at the Savoy. We arrived a little late, by design, and I had to be introduced to all the other lunching ladies.

I was surprised when Felicity introduced me by my married name. She stopped in front of the next lady and commented that we both had the same name.

'Oh, goodness,' she said, 'I believe you are related.'

This was my mother-in-law in the flesh. She was more than a little surprised and so was I, but she turned to her neighbour at the table and said our marriage was all a long time ago!

After Peter's death, or probably before, she had ensured that none of his assets would pass to me. Not that I wanted any, but it confirmed my impression of her as a mother-in-law to be missed.

It took me a long time to come to terms with the whole episode, and I thought a complete change of scene and occupation might be the answer.

That was when I decided to return to the Territory. I needed a job with a challenge and knew I could find it there.

BACK TO THE TERRITORY

Jenny's parents had returned from their visit to Malaysia. They were shocked at the way my life had changed during their time away, but their return made it easier for me to leave Perth behind and start a new chapter.

During all the above saga, Jenny was still in Vietnam with Save The Children and had become involved with David, whom she later married.

I applied for a position as a school health nurse based in Darwin again.

The town had grown considerably since I left in 1966, but it was still rather primitive in parts.

The health department offices were housed in tin huts on the Esplanade, which was still undeveloped bush on top of the cliffs.

The office of the director of health was in an elevated house in the middle of the huts. He had a wall air conditioner, no one else did. We had overhead fans, and everyone had a collection of rocks or heavy items to hold their paperwork in place.

Dr Helen Phillips oversaw the school health section, and we had several other doctors join us to assist with the growing workload as new suburban schools opened.

Apart from visiting schools to check the general health of the children and deal with the ever-present head lice infestations, we administered all the infant immunisations at various infant health clinics in the Darwin area.

We also did audiometric testing on the children. At times we also did health and hearing checks at bush schools, but we never managed to visit all the schools on our patch.

I decided to buy a car soon after arrival back in Darwin. I settled on a second-hand VW Beetle and christened it 'Charles.' The first time I drove it into town I parked in the parking lot outside the Woolworth store and then went up Smith Street to do some shopping. I met a friend by chance, and we had coffee.

We wended our way back down the street, stood at the bus stop as usual and caught the bus home. We were halfway there when I suddenly remembered I had driven into town. I kept quiet, put my shopping in my room and then walked back into town to rescue Charles.

We used our own cars to travel to the town schools and received a small travel allowance for it. Keeping a logbook for reimbursement helped me keep track of my use as the car did not have a petrol gauge!

When I bought it, George of Continental Motors gave me an idea of the range usual on a full tank and showed me an extra pedal on the floor that could be flipped over to give me about thirty kilometres more.

Sometime after I started using the car for work, two of us were going to the same school for the morning, so Mary asked if I would like to go with her in her brand-new VW car. Of course!

We went out to the Esplanade and got into her car, but when she turned the key, there was no engine sound. She muttered something about the battery, got out, lifted the back seat and fiddled with something that I couldn't quite see from where I sat. She returned to her seat, turned the key, engine fired, and we were off. I waited until I got home that night before I lifted the backseat in Charles and there was his battery. Just as well that I did as it had been leaking acid which had eroded a considerable bit of the car floor.

Back to see George again. While his workers shored up the battery to ensure it wouldn't fall into the road on the next rough bush track I drove on, George gave me a much-needed lesson in basic car 'housekeeping.'

Our 'patch' included all schools in the Top End, down as far as Newcastle Waters. We hosted visits from staff of the Commonwealth Acoustic Laboratory from Adelaide three times a year to retest children we had earmarked for their attention and issue bone conduction hearing aids to those who needed them.

On some of these visits we also 'caught a lift' on aerial medical planes to bush schools. When other health staff heard where we were heading for the next trip, they often gave us cash for a pandanus fibre basket, a particular kind of carving or bark painting depending on our destination. Different areas were renowned for particular crafts. If we were going to Milingimbi, colleagues requested mud crabs!

We always took our own lunches and stocked up on little luxuries for the health staff working in remote places. Fresh fruit was always very welcome, and if we had been lucky enough to find a Sara Lee cheesecake it was a feast day.

After I had been working there for two months, the woman who trained me, Heather, had to transfer to Adelaide to care for her sick mother, which meant I had to step up and help recruit and train other staff.

Sometime in 1973 it was decided to invest in a proper soundproof booth for us to do our audio work in.

This arrived as a flat pack with less than explicit instructions, so the construction was a bit fraught to say the least. Space for its construction was limited as well. To enter the booth, people had to walk down a dark alley and past the door. If the door was open it blocked the alley. However, we appreciated its addition to our tools.

When the whole thing had to be deconstructed to be taken to the department's new home in the Mutual Life Company (MLC) building, they had to be very particular regarding its placement as it was lead-lined and very heavy.

There were no businesses dealing in hearing aids in Darwin, so pensioners and others with hearing loss missed out unless they went to another state where they could have audiometric testing and buy a hearing aid if they could afford one. Toward the end of 1973, I was invited to go to Adelaide to the Commonwealth Acoustic Laboratory (CAL) offices to be taught better techniques for the testing. I also learnt how to make ear moulds using the kind of paste dentists use to mould gums for dentures. When I returned to Darwin another nurse had been added to our staff, so I was able to find time to test a few pensioners and make ear moulds to send with their audiogram to businesses that supplied hearing aids. Not ideal by any means, but a step forward for some of them.

When I was on leave in Perth, I walked the streets and went into all the stores that dealt in hearing aids to explain the difficulties for deaf people other than children in Darwin.

I asked if any of them could think of a solution, and Laubman and Pank offered to review any audiograms I sent, and if I could include an ear mould, they might be able to help. They sent the hearing aids to me, and I supervised the introduction to the person involved.

Several pensioners acquired hearing aids in this manner, and Laubman and Pank opened their own shop in Darwin soon after, so I felt the effort was well worth it.

Meanwhile, Dr Phillips had been campaigning hard to persuade Ear Nose and Throat (ENT) specialists from other states to visit the Territory to examine some of our most urgent cases. One specialist came up from Adelaide, but he was unwilling to operate as we had no real control over the pre-operative or post-operative care of the children brought in from outstations.

However, one specialist from Melbourne was willing to operate. The children involved were all from bush locations, so it was a matter of arranging their travel and finding them suitable accommodation. Add to this the fact that the surgical teams at Darwin Hospital did not want to give up any of their theatre time either. We quite often had to bargain with Hildegard, the sister in charge of the operating theatres. However, they all benefitted in the end as the Melbourne ENT surgeon was instrumental in procuring an operating microscope for the theatre.

In May 1974, Dr Phillips died following a recurrence of a previous brush with cancer.

Her position was filled by Dr Tek Lam who had a strong interest in health education, which was added to our task list. Dr Soong was also employed by the department as a health educator.

He organised a weekend retreat to Batchelor for teenagers. They were given talks and demonstrations of healthy living at the retreat, and I was recruited to be the chaperone in the girls' accommodation.

No stimulants of any kind were allowed, so no tea or coffee, and no cigarettes or alcohol. It was not exactly a resounding success, and it was never repeated.

However, Dr Soong decided I might be able to help him further. He was keen to find out where drugs were bought and sold amongst other things.

There was a late-night coffee stand in Mitchell Street that he found of particular interest. I had long hair, so he asked me to leave it loose, dress a bit 'hippish,' and lurk there to see if I could find out anything about the drug trade!

I loitered at Rocky's Place on several evenings. I never had any offers of drugs, but I got several offers for other services, so I declined to carry on this undercover work.

By the end of 1973 'community nursing' was the topic of the day. We had been doing that for years, but under separate banners.

There were sections dealing with home nursing, infant health, a tuberculosis team, a leprosy team, and a roving bush nursing team. They each had their own speciality, but they were able to co-operate and share a lot of information. Now it was suggested that as from a certain date, community nursing would be the name of the game.

The officials organising all this presumed that everyone was well-equipped to deal with all aspects of community nursing, not just their speciality, so there was a lot of uncertainty and unrest in the air. Several of us expressed our thoughts on the change, including myself.

I was asked to go to the office of the departmental head. I knew him as I had recently house sat for him while he took his family to Fiji for a holiday. He wanted me to go down to Katherine and take over the hospital for a year because the matron who was there was going on study leave. I replied that I hadn't been inside a hospital for several years and wouldn't know how to manage one.

'Just look fierce and growl now and then. You'll be all right,' he said.

It seemed if you were a potential troublemaker, the department thought of a way to give you something else to worry about.

During my time as a school health nurse, I was living in the hospital Annexe together with other non-hospital staff, which included some aerial medical staff. At weekends they had to be on-call for emergencies, and I often volunteered to take third call. This meant I did quite a few trips out to communities, mostly to pick up sick children and their mothers. Because of this, I got to know one of the pilots quite well and we began going out together now and then.

One day I mentioned I would love to be able to fly. Not long after this, Paul 'borrowed' a Cessna several times and took great delight in showing me how to fly it. We flew to the other side of the harbour where there were a couple of old airstrips no longer in use. We would fly low and 'buzz' the strip to alarm any animals that might be lurking there. That is where he taught me to land and take off, and then he handed me the control for the flight back to Darwin. I knew I could not afford proper lessons, and I would be handicapped because of my poor sight, but it was great fun.

Then it got even better.

Paul belonged to the local parachute club (not called skydivers in those days).

He took me to Batchelor and introduced me to the others. It was not long before I was going up for the ride and then after a few more lessons I was persuaded to do a jump. I did a total of four jumps, but on the last one I twisted an ankle badly so that put me out of action for a while.

By the time I was agile again, Paul had a new girlfriend. I had to admit I didn't really mind, as jumping out of planes was a bit too risky for me.

Later, a group of us went to the local rodeo, and that was where I met Geoff. He worked for the primary industry department and was very involved in a tick eradication project, which involved working with buffalo.

Wanting to impress me no doubt, he invited me to go with him to Berrimah Farm to see how they got the blood samples from the buffalo.

He armed himself with the syringe and sample bottles and off we went to face the beasts! Several of his mates were hanging around, I guess, to see how I would react to all of this.

Geoff had three tries on one beast and still hadn't got a sample. I felt sorry for the poor animal, so I took the syringe, looked the animal in the eye, told it that it would all be over in the shake of a guinea pigs' tail and got the blood sample. After that, I was welcome any time they were engaged in that task. Shortly after this, Geoff was offered a post down in Tennant Creek and tried to persuade me to move there. By then I had Katherine on my map, and even though that was a challenge, I preferred it to Tennant Creek.

While I was living in the hospital annexe, three of us went to cake decorating classes that were held in the local high school in the evenings. We all discovered different talents at this. Yvonne was the expert at piping icing lace, my forte was making small flowers in fondant icing, and Dawn was the expert fondant icing maker. It wasn't long before we were taking commissions for cakes. Our pièce de resistance was being asked to ice a three-tiered wedding cake. This was in May when rains had ceased, and the air was dry. We set about it and had the three cakes completed. The wedding was to be held on Saturday, and a very large storm broke over Darwin on Thursday night.

The humidity was 100%, and when we checked the cakes on Friday morning, they were a sorry sight. All the lace work had sagged beyond repair, my flowers were ruined and even the fondant was perspiring.

Disaster! But never say die; so, we set about sorting it out. First job was to scrape off all the decorations, then dry the fondants as much as possible. Meantime, the cleaning lady of the annexe came to our rescue by allowing us to use a spare room and summoning a bunch of extension cords. We arranged the cakes on the bed and cranked the overhead fan to full blast.

We borrowed everyone's bedside light and placed them, so they were shining down on the cakes and helping to dry the fondant. The corridor outside our rooms was a mass of electric cables.

Then we rushed off to work. Once home in the afternoon, we began the task of remaking iced lace and flowers while Dawn repaired the fondant. By 4:00 am on the Saturday morning we had it all assembled once again.

After a couple of hours sleep, we arranged to deliver it to the reception hall. We commandeered three friends with cars, one cake on the lap of one of us in each car. Then a very stately procession to the hall where we handed over the cakes and a few spare bits of lace if needed. We heaved a collective sigh of relief and vowed on the spot never to do it again.

We still received requests for iced cakes, and I specialised in children's birthday cakes for a while. In those days they were not the elaborate constructions they are today. It was quite usual for me to use a packet mix to bake a cake as soon as I got home on Friday afternoon, hold it under a fan to get it cool enough to ice and add jellybeans or smarties or whatever had been requested and then deliver it on Saturday morning. In some ways, my move to Katherine was a blessing as I found cake decorating quite a chore for very little reward.

KATHERINE REVISITED

I ARRIVED BACK IN KATHERINE in February 1974. I did my best to find out how the hospital operated and to get to know my staff.

I was almost immediately summoned to a meeting at the district officer's office to discuss the possibility of the town being flooded by the Katherine River.

It was decided that in the event of flooding, the hospital would be moved to the old air force base at Tindal. Two of the buildings out there had already been surveyed as suitable, and it was up to the hospital staff to make them habitable!

They had been unused and abandoned for years, so I accompanied the hospital secretary and some of the hospital cleaning staff out to do an inspection.

We spent the rest of the day cleaning with brooms and mops as best we could, and we were assured that the power would be turned on later. We were tired, filthy, and very hungry as we travelled back to town in the dark. After I had showered, I went over to the hospital to assess the situation there.

Some patients had already been discharged, and the remainder had all their important paperwork, some medications and their personal belongings attached to the ends of their beds in pillowcases ready for a swift uplift if deemed necessary. All of this had been organised by the medical super and his offsider.

I went over to my flat around midnight and lay on the bed with my essentials also in a pillowcase ready for a quick exit if required.

The next morning, I woke later than usual and looked out of my bedroom window to see the river swirling along at a great speed but still within its banks.

I went across to the hospital to be told that the peak had passed, and we would stay put!

Huge sigh of relief all round, but the river had flooded the road out to Tindal, so all the supplies that had been ferried out there in readiness for evacuation were now stranded out there.

The kitchen staff were at their wit's end as they didn't have enough food in the larder for lunch that day, so the hospital secretary made an urgent phone call to stores in Katherine asking them to fill the gap.

Quite an eventful introduction and a good way to find out who was who in the hierarchy of the town.

The native ward was gone, but the original maternity ward was still there with an outpatient area, a men's ward and one for the children. As for looking fierce and growling now and then, I took a leaf, as it were, from Miss Brennan's book.

She had arrived at Darwin Hospital from Alice Springs late in 1965. She had no idea what was going on, so to find out what made the place tick around the clock, she used to do rounds in full starched regalia, morning, noon, and night-time too. Shortly after her arrival, I was on night duty in casualty at Darwin Hospital. There were no patients at the time. I was in the sisters' office sewing up my shoes because Les Heaven, the only shoe shop in town, didn't have any more in my size. I heard the front door bang followed by quick, bouncy footsteps. It registered in my mind that whoever it was they were not too sick because they were moving well. I looked up and there was Miss Brennan standing in the doorway.

'Good morning,' she said.

'Good morning, Matron.'

'What are you doing?'

No point in trying to fluff this one. I told her I was sewing up my shoes and why, so she came over and taught me how to do a better knot.

'And don't pick up that phone,' she said as she helped me.

'No, Matron.'

She didn't want me to warn the rest of the hospital she was on the way.

To find out how Katherine Hospital ticked, I did am, pm and night-time rounds, but not in full regalia. It proved to be a very good ploy as it gave staff on other shifts, some of them permanent night staff, a chance to have their say.

On the occasions when I arrived to find some drama unfolding, I would take over the mundane tasks and leave the duty staff to work as they would if I was not there.

I had also decided that honesty was the best policy, so soon after my arrival I informed my senior staff that I was not up to speed on the latest techniques or laboratory findings and would be glad if they would please teach me.

I think they were a bit shocked, but they rose to the occasion very well. I was brought up to speed in all kinds of things and was soon popping in sutures and setting up drips just as well as the rest of them.

At various times we would be allocated a new locum or registrar. When this happened in the wet season, it was a lifeline to all the old boys who liked their grog and usually slept rough.

They would come up to the outpatients, coughing and wheezing and limping and telling all kinds of stories to the new chum doctor, and they would often persuade him to admit them for investigation.

A roof over their head, three meals a day, somebody to wait on them—what more could you ask for?

When it was getting to the stage of not having a spare bed or two, I'd go to the medical superintendent of the day and ask if he would cast an eye over the motley crew to see which of them could be safely turfed out. When I appeared in the men's ward the next day, I'd tell everyone we had visitors coming from Canberra and we wanted the place to look nice, so how about an emu parade.

I would hand out big garbage bags to everyone, keep one for myself and chivvy the ones we wanted to go, out to start collecting the rubbish. About fifteen minutes later, someone would call me to the telephone (or something to get me out of there). Some of the lingerers would go before lunch, some later, and if their bed wasn't slept in that night they were discharged. They all knew the drill. I can't imagine doing that today!

SHROVE TUESDAY, ROLLERSKATES AND BLOOD SUPPLIES

THE HOSPITAL ALWAYS CELEBRATED SHROVE TUESDAY with pancake races between the patients and staff of the men's and children's wards.

One year we had everything all lined up for the 'off'. The batter was made and resting when the hospital secretary came to my office and said we would have to cancel pancakes because Mr So-and-so has driven down from Darwin, and he'd brought a visitor from Canberra. That was very unusual because the Canberra visitors usually waited until the dry season.

'We can't,' I said. 'The batter is made. Who did you say had driven down?'

I happened to know he considered himself quite a big wheel in the Anglican congregation in Darwin, so he'd know all about Shrove Tuesday.

I went along to the medical superintendent's office, tapped on the door, and introduced myself.

'Now, Gentlemen,' I said, 'it is Shrove Tuesday, the day before Ash Wednesday. In fact, it's a celebration day before we go into Lent. The pancakes are waiting to be tossed. Now which of you is the best tosser? Do come along and show us how.'

They had a lovely time. I often wonder what comments they made about it later.

When the new ward was built, I jokingly commented that now the place was bigger I'd need roller-skates to get around. On Christmas morning, I was called to the new ward where the staff presented me with a pair of roller-skates.

It was many moons since I had worn skates of any kind, but I strapped them on, sent up a silent prayer and I did two lengths of the long corridor without falling flat on my face.

After that, I used to whiz along the Gorge Road at night under the moon and stars. In those days there wasn't very much in the way of night traffic there.

The only real hazard during the dry season was the number of large pythons lying on the road absorbing the warmth, but they were very pretty, and I enjoyed the impromptu obstacle course.

During the wet season, the health inspector and I would drive out along the Gorge Road, pull off the road and park with the headlights still shining. Then we used our homemade butterfly nets to collect some of the bugs that flew into the light. We'd pop them in jars and take them home to examine under a microscope before letting them fly off again.

We never found anything that was particularly rare, but some of them were beautiful.

The hospital also ran its own blood bank. That is, we would bleed as we needed. This was easy to organise for pre-booked surgery because we had a list of people of different blood groups to call upon. One Christmas Eve we admitted a man with a depressed skull fracture who had lost a lot of blood. A surgeon was being flown down from Darwin to operate, and we needed blood.

Fortunately, the town still had a switchboard, so I phoned and asked them to scour the various parties to find the people I needed to donate a pint. We had 100% roll up, plus several extras who were keen to donate even if they weren't the right blood group. The patient had his Christmas drinks dripped into him, but he survived.

TRANSPORTING PATIENTS

BEFORE THE AIRPORT was moved out to Tindall, having it right next to the hospital was a great help sometimes.

We often had patients in hospital, especially mothers with children, and it was hard to find transport to get them back to their community. However, most of the stations had light planes and would come into town now and then.

I would wander down to the camp, find the old men with whom I got on very well and ask them to let me know when such and such a station plane came in, which they did.

Then I would contact the town switchboard and ask them to track the pilot, find where he was going and ask him to phone us with a view to getting the patients repatriated.

Soon after arriving back at Katherine Hospital, I found out that Sister Eperjesy was in charge at Bamyili. I had met this lady at various summer schools initiated by the Territory Branch of the College of Nursing in previous years. She was not a character to be messed with. I decided to phone her and ask if we could meet

184

in Bamyili so I could see what facilities she had. It was a good move, and we established a fruitful working relationship with neither of us being too fussed about doing everything by the book.

Later she and husband Zollie took over the health clinic at Pine Creek, so we often met up in the wee small hours of the morning on a roadside to take a road accident victim from her ambulance to the Katherine one.

You can bet that while she was getting her supplies ready, Zollie had been busy making a thermos of coffee. We really appreciated it during very cold nights.

AERIAL MEDICAL SERVICES – AN EVACUATION

At this time, the Aerial Medical Service was only based in Darwin, and if all their planes were busy, they would sometimes ask Katherine for help.

Fortunately, the local air charter operator was very generous and diverted his planes quite often. He also organised special trips for us.

Some of his planes were single-engine jobs, and health department employees were not covered by departmental insurance for single-engine travel.

As most of my staff were either young things or married with families, I decided I was the most expendable. I did just about all the escort jobs, but I had some fun.

One of the funniest events occurred when we were asked to pick up a lass who had fallen from her horse. She was on a station I was not familiar with.

It was late afternoon, so we had to get a wriggle on to do it before last light. Single engine, new pilot, and the only thing I knew about him was that his wife was expecting twins. We flew on and on looking for the landing strip. Eventually we spotted it, landed, and then taxied around for a quick take-off.

Usually when you turn the plane engine off in these situations, you hear the station vehicle chugging along toward you. There was dead silence. A bit later we heard a Ute chugging along. A fellow arrived and said, 'G'day,' obviously wondering what we were doing there. We told him.

It turned out we were at the wrong station on the wrong strip. The other station was over the escarpment. By this time, it was too dark to take off safely because it was prime wallaby time.

'You'd better come up to the house, the missis is getting tea,' he said.

We piled into the Ute and went up to the house where his partner was getting tea ready. She nearly died with surprise when she saw me because she knew that I knew she was married to someone else. She was supposed to be in Melbourne visiting her mother. We never said a word about this throughout the whole episode.

Our first job was to get to the radio and let Katherine know where we were.

We had to do it during the galah session (gossip time on the radio) when everybody was listening, so everybody knew we'd made a boo-boo. Never mind, stay the night. Well, we didn't have much choice! The lady of the house slapped a couple more steaks on the BBQ.

'The bathroom is out the back. There are a few browns [snakes] around, better watch it.'

They did have an inside toilet, so I decided I was clean enough and did not need the bathroom.

My hostess' young son was there so it was decided I could have his bed, and he could sleep on the settee. They put a trundle bed in front of the stove for the pilot.

This all happened in the middle of the dry, and it does get a tad chilly out there. My bed turned out to be a big double bed, but when it came to bedclothes, all I had was the equivalent of a 'grannie's knee rug' made from crocheted squares. During the night I was very tempted to creep out and ask the pilot to make room for me in front of the stove. I didn't know what his sense of humour was like, so I didn't do it.

We were off again at first light over the escarpment to find the lass had recovered enough and she really did not want to risk a trip with people who did not know where they were going!

OTHER EVACUATIONS

ON ANOTHER OCCASION, we flew down to Hooker Creek to pick up a mother and child. In those days, the end of the runway was very close to the settlement, so no actual ground transport was needed. We taxied to the end and turned for take-off as usual. However, there was a big gathering of people there and we wondered what was going on. The clinic staff rushed out and bundled the mother and child onboard.

'Get going, get going, get going!'

So, we did. The people in the mob were starting to bang the fuselage with sticks and nulla nullas. I never did find out what was going on, but we were very pleased to get out of it.

One Christmas morning we were asked to arrange to pick up a sick child from Hooker Creek please. I don't know why but there was only a single-engine plane available, so it took us all morning to get down there. We landed, taxied, and turned ready for take-off. The staff had just finished their Christmas dinner, but the patient was ready, so back to the plane. We were just about ready to turn the engine on when a small boy rushed onto the strip carrying a plastic bag. He climbed onto the wing and handed the bag to me saying, 'Sister thought you might like these.' After take-off, I looked in the bag to find two cans of hot Coca-Cola and a bag of salt and vinegar chips. That was lunch.

We were asked to deviate on the return trip to pick up another child at Nutwood Downs. We landed and taxied, turned and were ready to go. Usually on these trips I considered myself to be a fairy (fairies never need to 'go'), but this time I did. The end of the runway was near a group of shrubs, and I asked the woman who had delivered the mother and child to us whether there was a toilet anywhere near. She pointed me down a windy path to a small shed, but when I opened the door, I had to laugh. Sure, there was a proper toilet, but the whole place was stacked floor to ceiling with toilet rolls—the supply for the whole of the wet season. I had to back in to make use of the facility.

The army used to (and probably still do) hold exercises in the Katherine area each dry season and call up the reserves for training. Dr Mahajani, a surgeon based in Darwin, was one of their reserves. He was an eager recruit, but he always came to the hospital to beg for extra blankets for his cot bed. There were never enough for him. He introduced us to Major George who oversaw the whole army exercise. On one occasion, we were desperate for a plane to pick up a labouring lass out at Pigeonhole Station—we just could not raise a plane anywhere. I thought to ask Major George, so I had the hospital secretary ring him.

'Not a problem,' he said.

In next to no time, I was on my way to the airport and put aboard a Pilatus Porter plane—almost vertical take-off and landing. Not for the fainthearted, but I had been forewarned. We eventually found the station runway. We landed in similar fashion, almost straight down. The poor mother-to-be was in shock about this strange plane, but she waited until we got to the ambulance before she delivered.

KATHERINE LIFE

Living in Katherine wasn't all work and no play, although it could be lonely at times. I felt I was on-call whenever I was in town. I had friends among the staff, but I trod a fine line because I may have to reprimand or discipline them further down the line.

There were always street stalls outside Katherine stores on Saturday. No matter who was collecting for what, I contributed by providing cakes and biscuits or buying them.

The hospital social club organised a fundraising gorge walk, a midnight marathon. We set off from the post office at midnight and walked to the gorge. The club supplied breakfast and transported us back to town. It was 59km, so quite a trek.

We did it again the following year on bicycles. It was great fun because we had brilliant starlight and could watch satellites going over. In those days, there was very little traffic but always the possibility of a python or two.

I used to visit long-time friend Frank Lansdowne at his shack above the actual Knots Crossing of the

Katherine River. His shack was about half a kilometre along the riverbank from the hospital. He would offer me a drink, a very generous pour of sweet sherry over a glass full of shaved ice. He was the only man I knew who had a big block of ice, and he would shave it off as needed. We would discuss the world of the day, and he would enlighten me about the world of his day. It was very interesting.

When I started producing mango wine, I used to share that too. I had one particularly good vintage, and I sold some of it to Colin Jack-Hinton who used to visit Frank. Some vintages were better than others. I went there down a little track on my bicycle, and I'm sure I could have been caught for being drunk in charge of a bicycle several times, but I always made it home safely!

Christmas 1974 saw Darwin almost destroyed by Cyclone Tracy. The hospital secretary was the first to receive the news, and we all sprang into action. Supplies of mattresses, linen and medical items had been stored in part of the new mortuary, and these were loaded up to be sent north. As was usual at Christmas time, only patients who required our care were housed in the hospital, so we had a few empty beds. We had no real idea of what to expect, so we waited anxiously until the first refugees began to arrive in town. Some of these were health department staff who needed accommodation while they tried to sort out how to maintain health services.

The old nurses' quarters, where the health inspector and I were the only occupants, was taken over. They placed mattresses on the floor of the lounge room, and people slept there day and night. No frills, but it was a roof over their heads, a mattress to sleep on, overhead fans and food on a twenty-four-hour basis.

As for the actual nursing side of things, we were kept busy too. At one time the police were limiting the number of cars they allowed into town, advising them to fill up with petrol and food and keep going. The Country Women's Association (CWA) and other organizations swung into action with tea and sandwiches galore.

As arrivals at the hospital increased, we triaged as they came through the door. Most requests were for tetanus injections, followed by lacerations requiring suturing. Some required X-rays to be taken with access to the medical staff.

Those receiving tetanus injections were supplied with their personal record, and only those requiring more treatments were issued with a hospital record. There was no way we could have written full records for everyone, especially since this was likely to be their one and only visit to Katherine Hospital.

I was busy suturing a man's hand, but his main concern was for his cat. They had it in their car, and, naturally, it was very upset. He wondered if we had any sedative for such things! The doctor, who was treating someone in the next cubicle overheard this conversation and said he could probably help. There was a small amount of soluble phenobarbitone in the drug cupboard in Outpatients that he thought was past its use-by date for giving to small children. He asked the weight of said cat, calculated what he thought would be a safe dose, and we went out to the car and dosed the cat. They were going to drive over to Kununurra. About a week later, the man returned to have his sutures removed. I hardly dared ask about the cat, as in the meantime the local vet had told us that we had probably overdosed it quite a bit. I plucked up courage and was told that the cat had slept through the whole trip. They had given her fluids using an ear dropper on the way, and she was now settled in her new home.

The stream of survivors slowed down to a trickle, and life returned to some normality.

I had to vacate the flat I had been living in for the return of the real matron. As I would be on the move myself within a couple of days, I moved into a corridor with a mattress. I used the filing cabinets that were being stored there to secure some privacy.

Jane was not impressed when she heard that we had not created full records for everyone and was concerned we would never know how many doses of this and that had been given. That one was easily solved by looking at the records of what had been in stock, what had been imported over that period and what was left on hand. I just felt that people were more important than records that would never be accessed again cluttering up the shelves. Just as well I was leaving as I don't think we would have worked well together.

Toward the end of that first year, I had been approached regarding the allocation of a scholarship to go to Melbourne for a year to further my education by studying administration. The previous matron at Katherine had been there during this year and would be returning to re-commence her work there, so this was an opportune moment for me to study.

After a farewell dinner hosted by Mike the health inspector and another friend, we were all a little tipsy. They asked me if there was anything I would like to do before I left town. We were sitting in the car outside the hotel. There was a building across the street that had a flight of shallow steps down to the pavement. The top of these steps was accessed by a laneway behind. Mike drove us onto the laneway, and we bumped our way down the steps; great fun but not to be attempted during daylight hours. Then we drove to the hospital secretary's home. He used to ride his bicycle to work each day. We stole his bike, and Darcy and I held it outside the car as we drove back to the hospital. Then the two men hoisted it on the ropes to the top of the flagstaff in front of the hospital. Someone finally noticed it around ten in the morning, but we never confessed as to how it got there.

MELBOURNE, HERE I COME

THEN IT WAS OFF TO MELBOURNE in January 1975. I drove down to Alice Springs and boarded the train to Port Augusta. A couple of people who were refugees from Darwin but staying in Katherine asked if I could deliver a couple of packages on my way to Melbourne.

One of these was to a policeman stationed at Port Augusta, so once the cars were unloaded from the train, I drove into the little town to find the police station and somewhere to stay the night. My car had been one of the last to be unloaded, so by the time I was mobile all the other cars had gone, and all the motels had No Vacancy signs lit up.

At the police station I gave my name and the fact that I had a package for one of their officers. Apparently, he had alerted them to my possible arrival, but he was home asleep. The fellow in charge of the station for the night enquired as to where I would be staying, and when he heard about the motels being full, he offered me a bed, of sorts, at the station.

After giving me tea and toast, I was shown to the watchhouse cell. There was a thin mattress and pillow and a blanket, so I spent the night there. In the morning I handed the package over and then my saviour of the night took me to his home where I could have a shower. His wife gave me a good breakfast to see me on my way.

Driving across country took me the whole day, and I finally arrived at Mildura, the destination for the second package. It was early evening, and I found the motel where I had to deliver to the manager. He was delighted to see me. Although all their regular rooms were booked for the night, he insisted I must stay overnight, and he would see me in the dining room later to have dinner with him. That is how I came to spend the night in their honeymoon suite!

Very luxurious after the previous night in a police cell. Over dinner, the manager asked if I had any idea what I had brought to him. I had no clues. He told me the package contained the most valuable items of the stock from Darwin's best jewellery shop. The manager of the shop thought it would be best to get it in safe hands down south when he didn't have access to a proper safe himself. Just as well I didn't know, as I would have worried about making safe contact.

I managed to find a small flat within walking distance from the college in Melbourne. There was off street parking for the car, so I was very fortunate.

I don't remember much about the content of the course, but I realised they were teaching the ideal of good management, which had to be trimmed to fit in remote locales.

There were twenty-four students, a mixed bunch with a few men included.

I gathered that none of my fellow students had any practical experience in hospital administration, so I considered myself to be very fortunate.

We spent most of one morning being advised on the best practice for selection of staff. At the end of the session, Margaret, our tutor, who knew I had had a year of practical experience, asked me if the content of the lecture bore any resemblance to real practice.

I entertained the class by retailing just one incident during my time in Katherine. A staff member phoned in to tell me she could not work her afternoon shift. As was usual in country towns, we never had 'spare' staff, and most of the local staff were young married women with families, so it was difficult for them to do a double shift.

I was reallocating some of my tasks for the day so I could do the afternoon shift when a lady arrived at my office door. She very politely asked if she could have a brief look over the hospital. She was a registered nurse on her way to Darwin to work, but she thought Katherine might be a nice spot when she had finished in Darwin.

I gave her the deluxe tour and had her signed up before lunch. She did the afternoon shift and many more besides. She also had experience in ICU and operating theatre work, so proved to be a welcome asset who shared her knowledge with the rest of the nursing staff and me. We still meet now and then as she now lives in Darwin and never left the Territory.

During the college course we were deployed to other establishments to witness different styles of management, so another student and I drove to Adelaide for three weeks to spend time at the Children's Hospital there.

By now I had realised that I was very fortunate to be studying under a Commonwealth scholarship. Apart from my study costs, it also paid most of the rental on the flat and any travel I undertook related to the course.

Some of the other the students were also attending on scholarships, but others were working part-time doing evening and night shifts at weekends to be able to make up for loss of full-time work.

During my year in Melbourne, I was out and about most weekends doing the usual tourist things. I often visited Prahran market late on Saturday mornings when the stall holders would be selling their wares at reduced prices.

Apart from fruit and vegetables, I usually came home with a big bunch of fresh flowers. We relied on overhead fans for cooling in the Territory, so cut flowers did not survive very long.

I also enjoyed the free entertainment offered throughout the summer by the city council in parks and plazas. My flat was literally just around the corner from gardens and parks, which meant I could walk through them if I was going to the city.

BACK TO KATHERINE

Taking the train from Melbourne to Port Augusta I faced the long drive back to Katherine. This was in early December and there were several quite difficult creek crossings on the way. I was fortunate that there were also others traveling and at times we waited to make sure that people following forded the creeks without mishap.

When I returned to Katherine in 1976 after my year in Melbourne, I attended an evening pottery class at the local high school. I enjoyed it and wanted to continue working with clay.

At that time, many things that were not readily available in town were brought up from Adelaide by Bulls' Bus Service.

Bringing slabs of prepared clay in this way was rather expensive due to its weight, however, one of the hospital orderlies told me of what he thought was a seam of white clay about thirty kilometres out of town on the road toward Darwin. I drove out one Saturday to investigate and found what appeared to be workable, albeit dry, clay. I took some home, puddled it and made a couple of slab-built dishes. I persuaded one of the high school teachers to place them in the school kiln for the next firing. My clay bisque fired to a pale salmon pink colour.

Then I negotiated with the hospital secretary of the day for use of part of the old mortuary as my pottery workshop.

Since the new one had been built, this structure had been left unused. It had power and access to water, and due to its previous history as a mortuary was unlikely to be wanted by anyone else.

I organised for an electric wheel and a gas-fired kiln to be sent up from Adelaide. I would drive out to my clay source some weekends, dig it out and go home with my car boot loaded with buckets of dry clay. I laid it on a tarpaulin, put on my wooden clogs and trampled all over it to reduce the lumps. Then I would sieve it to remove pebbles and grit, add water to create my clay.

I could usually be found up to the ears in clay creations on the evenings and weekends. I also used to visit Ruth, Frank's daughter, who also lived on the riverbank further up a dirt road. She was a potter of some note and became a valuable mentor in the world of clay. She was also a good friend and someone I could talk with about many things.

My position as matron of the hospital meant that I felt I had to be careful in my friends. I could only be friendly up to a point with my senior staff, and while I was friendly to all, close friendship was dicey.

Ruth and I had two exhibitions and sales each year in a shed near old Frank's home, and we usually sold out each time.

I can't remember exactly when it happened, but an establishment opened in town that sported a gym, a spa, and a roller-skating rink. Ruth and I discussed this and decided to find out for ourselves what it was all about.

They had a ladies day/evening once a week, so we sallied forth. We were introduced to all the wonderful machinery in the gym and advised to go round doing twenty movements at each station.

We cut that back to ten and found ourselves at the entrance to the spa at the end, so on the spur of the moment we decided to give that a try too.

There were cubicles for our clothes, so we stripped off completely and went into the actual spa room.

There were two ladies already up to their necks in bubbles, so we slipped into the water on the other side and relaxed nicely.

When the original two decided to get out we found they were both wearing bathing costumes. That explained the surprise on their faces as we walked in, no doubt.

We drip dried, dressed, and left, wondering how our appearance in the buff would be noised abroad! Not that we were worried.

However, the following week, someone else visiting the gym and surrounds informed us that there was a large notice at the front counter stating that bathing attire must be worn in the spa.

A similar situation today, we would probably have been displayed to the world on social media.

I attended the Anglican church in town, which was under the care of Brother Mark. He was a member of the Brotherhood of St Lawrence, and prior to his posting to Katherine had been a bush brother who travelled all round the Territory.

One of the conditions of belonging to the brotherhood was that the men remain single. However, Mark developed a fondness for the theatre sister at the hospital, and they began to see more of each other.

Their romance was rather hampered because they didn't want to jeopardise his position, and they knew tongues would wag if they were seen together too often. When I became aware of this situation, I found a way to divert the town gossips by arranging to visit spots with Mark where we were sure to be noted.

I'm not quite sure how the town classified me when it came to romance, but this was a good red herring while the actual romance proceeded.

Mark had trained as an accountant prior to joining the brotherhood, so after the wedding they both moved to Darwin where he began his accountancy practice again.

The next September, the whole town missed Mark. He used to organise a monster wine and cheese evening in the church grounds on a certain weekend each year. It took a deal of planning for such a wide variety of cheeses and wines to arrive in town when they were needed, and it was an event not to be missed.

Another church-related activity occurred when the ladies of the parish decided to open an opportunity shop.

Apart from whatever was collected or donated locally, several parishes in NSW and Victoria sent boxes of clothes for our shop.

We had next to nothing in the way of shop fittings, so there were tea chests dotted around all labelled with whatever was supposed to be inside. Those with long legs and arms were at a distinct advantage as they could reach to the bottom to find whatever gem was hidden there, and there were times when small people had to be rescued.

We also collected things for a varied boxful to send up to Pine Creek where a group of women distributed them.

In this way, our castoff clothes usually ended up in the Pine Creek box, so there was less likelihood of meeting someone wearing your dress coming toward you on Katherine Terrace.

Some of the contents of the boxes from other parishes were highly unsuitable for the tropics, so we would repack them and send to the parish in Alice Springs where it gets very chilly during the dry season.

Having already spent a year as matron at Katherine, I didn't find it too difficult to settle in again and tackle the daily challenges that life threw our way.

There were days when we shuddered if a tourist bus pulled into the parking lot. At times it was just the odd tourist who required our attention, but there were days when half the busload would descend on us with a variety of complaints. They expected instant attention and guaranteed remedies.

Then there were the rotating registrars. Most of them had never worked in a small country establishment before and had expectations of instant access to treatments and laboratory tests that were quite beyond our scope.

Maintaining my staff numbers was a constant problem. 'Touring' nursing staff were still in the habit of working in each setting for about six months, and if they escaped a serious romantic entanglement, it was time to try new pastures.

We mourned when some of them departed and waved farewell with a smile as others left, but there were many times when we would have been in trouble if we had had an influx of seriously ill patients.

If a patient required 'individual care,' it usually meant that I or someone else on the staff worked a double shift.

Around the end of 1976, the department employed a firm of management consultants to review working practices in all Territory hospitals.

It was an interesting exercise. I was tutored in the use of a particular calculator which was programmed to determine actual nursing hours required for the care of the patients in the beds.

My senior staff categorised their patients according to the set parameters, and I did the data entry.

It didn't make any difference to our staffing levels at the time, but it was a useful tool to demonstrate the need for a larger staff allocation in view of the workload. I was also taught the basics of introducing a quality control system throughout my nursing areas.

Until then, quality control measures had been considered vital, in central sterilising departments or laboratories, but they were not usual in ward situations.

I added to this by instigating evacuation and fire drills. These were not exactly popular, but the staff eventually began to feel proud of their speeds and offered suggestions for improvement.

I persuaded the hospital secretary to install similar programs in the catering and stores areas. Some of the findings were quite surprising.

The results of our labours were reported back to the consulting firm. They were suitably impressed, with the result that I was asked to work for them on several occasions in the future (with departmental blessing).

My role was mainly in what I call 'nursing ergonomics,' but I would occasionally be asked to investigate other ancillary areas. They also employed me for several studies in mental health facilities. I queried this, as I did not have any mental health qualifications.

Apparently, that was my best quality because when I saw something happening that I did not understand, I asked questions. Quite often, the answers I was given were not as they should have been.

It also gave me an insight into the plight of many patients in these establishments where the conditions were little short of Dickensian to my mind.

While working for them I became entangled with the CEO, and we began an affair that lasted over the next twenty-seven years. He was very happily married with family, and I did not want him on a permanent basis, so we enjoyed each other's company when we met up, usually while I was working for the firm.

In 1997, I returned to the UK for a short holiday. During that spell, I flew to Paris to join John, who had flown over to give a paper at a conference being held there. While he was conferring, I explored the city, and we went to a wonderful concert held in a cellar one evening. The instrument was a very old spinet that had to be tweaked and retuned between each movement, and no one moved or coughed for the whole evening. It was quite ethereal.

After the conference, we hired a car and drove down the Loire Valley. We visited all the wonderful chateaux and sampled the different cheeses and wines on our picnic lunches. Then we flew back to Heathrow, I went back to the village, and he took a plane back to Sydney. We went to New Zealand much later in our association, where I worked with him in a mental health facility in Dunedin.

Throughout our time together, we shared each other's highs and lows. In a sense, we acted as the 'devil's advocate' for each other.

His wife died after we had been associating for twenty-five years, and I later realised he wanted our association to be recognised by marriage. But by this stage in my life, I had accepted the fact that I wasn't capable of the complete love and surrender needed in such a relationship. I also knew I had not been his only 'other,' so I encouraged him to turn to Margaret. I received a photo of their wedding in Canada about a year later. I had no regrets and was happy he had company for the rest of his journey through life.

THE NEXT CHALLENGE

In July 1980, a new director of the health department visited Katherine Hospital on a junket to get to know the troops.

During the ritual BBQ, I was asked what I thought about computers in hospitals. We didn't have anything like that in the Territory, but I had certainly kept up to speed with developments elsewhere through my reading.

I reminded him that nurses were the ones who were in hospitals twenty-four hours a day, and if he wanted them to use computers, they had better be user-friendly.

That was the total of the discussion on computers. A couple of weeks later, I was invited back to Darwin to be the nursing representative on the Data Processing Committee—another steep learning curve, but a very interesting challenge.

It appeared that the invitation to Darwin was the result of my comment at the BBQ, but much later I discovered that moving me was a means of moving someone else into the Katherine position.

While it was a surprise at the time, when I gave it a bit of thought I realised I needed a change of occupation and location. Staying in a position because it's comfortable is not good for the organisation or the individual.

I had to pack up my life in Katherine in rather a hurry and find a new home for my cat, which was a hard thing for me.

Add that to the uncertainty as to what my life and duties were to be, and it was a very stressful time—it was a challenge.

The department found me a flat within walking distance of the offices. It was in a block that was partly occupied by office staff and other health-related workers.

I had no furniture of my own as I had always lived in accommodation provided since moving back to the Territory. The department supplied me with the essentials I requested, and I covered cardboard cartons with bits of material for occasional tables and bookshelves. It was enough until I found out what the job really entailed.

It would have been nice if the Data Processing Committee had been informed I was coming to join them, but I was taken to their next meeting and introduced as the nursing rep to join the team!

My welcome was less than overwhelming. They decided to give me the job they all hated—taking the minutes of their interminable meetings. While it was not my idea of fun either, it gave me a chance to catch up. Every time they mentioned a bit of computer jargon, they had to explain it to me.

They eventually accepted me, and I received an overview of what they were planning. I was up to date from reading my nursing journals and aware of how computing was being used in other hospitals all over the world, but my team seemed bent on reinventing the wheel in some respects.

Bearing in mind that there were hospitals in other states that were using computing programs that worked, it seemed logical to ask their advice and take advantage of their expertise, but the Territory team seemed determined to design screens and sequences fitted to the format and design of our paper forms.

It would have been much easier to adapt to a format that worked and alter the paper forms to suit, but I had the feeling that any idea of mine was bound to be ignored.

I was booked for a holiday to the UK soon after joining the team. Before I left, I arranged to see computer systems in Dundee, Scotland and in Whitechapel in the East end of London.

They were both generous with their time and gave me large wads of information about the systems. When

I returned, I offered all of this to the team and spoke about my visits, but they did not want to know!

Meantime, we were visiting all the hospitals in the Territory, measuring bench tops and storage spaces to make sure the video display units (VDU) and keyboards would fit.

The computer terminals were installed, and I was part of the team that had the task of teaching the hospital clerical staff to use them.

This was not easy because there were no drop-down menus, and there were several inconsistencies when moving from screen to screen. Many of the clerical staff were not even familiar with the keyboard. But we laboured on.

Then there was a wind of change throughout all the NT government departments. Up until then, they had operated on the division between Darwin and Alice Springs with Newcastle Waters being the mid-line.

Now the name of the game was 'Regionalisation.' There was no longer an NT Data Processing Team, and each region was to organise their own teams, so the Darwin team was downsized.

That left me out on a limb as far as a job went, but then I was assigned to assist the Territory chief nurse. I worked under her umbrella for several years, liaising with the Nurses' Registration Board, collecting, and collating a variety of statistics and producing annual reports.

Someone in the higher echelons of government suggested that now that we had computer access it would be wonderful to have a program available for all new recruits to the Territory to access information on services, population and where they could secure supplies in whatever community they would be stationed at.

It sounded great, but the logistics of such a program were mind-blowing. However, a committee was established, with representatives from all departments attending meetings.

I was dobbed in as the health rep. I tried valiantly to make sense of the discussions, but after the second meeting I noticed the representatives from many of the other departments changed each time we met, so there was very little continuity.

At the same time, I was assisting another senior nurse who was establishing actual locations, numbers of people and facilities available at all the outstations that were being set up by groups of Aboriginal people in their efforts to escape from the effects of heavy alcohol consumption in their communities.

This was another never-ending task as the people moved between groups or returned home and we had no way of knowing whether our information was up to date or not at any one time.

There were also changes being made within the department. With some people being relocated to the sixth floor of the building—unofficially known as 'Siberia.' As an outsider looking in, I found the selection of inmates for Siberia to be a very eclectic mix.

The chief pharmacist of the Territory was relocated there for a while. We had no idea why, but it didn't faze him at all. He was a bit of an entrepreneur and had his fingers in a lot of pies round town, so this just gave him more time to work on those. On the downside for him was the fact that he drove around in a bright red sports car, so actually locating him when he was needed was not too difficult.

Another inmate was a highly thought of radiographer. He was also a very skilled photographer, so he used his exile to spend more time collating his pictorial calendar for the next year.

Yet another was a doctor. I never discovered where he came from, but he was busy working on his thesis for another doctorate. He was writing longhand and wasn't allowed to use the typing pool in house, so I typed pages of his thesis when I wasn't being given much else to do. I did wonder if these moves were meant to encourage people to look for other employment, but they were all eventually gathered back into the fold.

Then I was informed I was to be attached to the Policy Review and Development section (PRD). The first policy I was given to investigate related to the medical kits supplied to outlying stations by the department. These kits were quite comprehensive in their contents, all of which were numbered.

If someone was sick on the station, they would be able to speak with a doctor via the radio telephone at certain times during the day, and if it was appropriate the doctor would prescribe an item from the kit.

This system was a godsend for remote cattle stations.

I winkled out the reason for the review from an overheard conversation in the office.

It appeared that someone of note from Canberra had been visiting a station and talking to the manager when one of the station hands interrupted to tell the manager that their prize bull had a nasty eye infection.

The manager told him to see his wife and ask her for the tube of eye ointment from the medical kit and use that on the bull.

That was the most sensible thing to do for people living in such remote places, as it might be several days before a vet could fly out.

The Canberra visitor did not see the logic of this; thus, we were asked to review our medical kit policy.

I advocated that we play for time and leave it alone. I've no idea of the result, but many of the requests for review were little more than nit picking by people who had never lived remotely.

When I arrived back in Darwin after my years in Katherine, I went to church as a way of getting in touch with the local community again. It wasn't long before I was on several rosters, from cleaning the cathedral to helping with after service coffee, singing in the choir, handing out hymn books and making loaves of vegemite sandwiches.

The parish assistant at the time was called Peter. He was tall and lanky and had a large black dog, aptly called 'Stinky,' who loved to sit in on services. Peter set up an early morning tea and coffee stall in the church grounds, and the long grassers of the day would come along for a hot drink and a sandwich to start their day.

'Long grasser' was the term used for the people, both aboriginal and European, who were usually heavy drinkers and preferred to sleep under the stars.

I went along to help quite often and got to know some of the regulars. One morning one of them told me he wouldn't be around for a while.

When I asked where he was going, he informed me 'Fannie Bay, of course!' With the wet season starting, he was planning to throw a brick through a window, get caught, be sent to Fannie Bay Jail for three months and get out in time for the next dry season. Accommodation and three meals a day for the duration.

Peter was also into gardening, and when he had a trailer full of rubbish to take to the tip, he'd ask if anyone would like the trip. We usually came back with the trailer full of stuff we had scavenged from the tip. It was a smelly, messy job but great fun.

One year, the choirmaster entered the cathedral choir in the local eisteddfod. We practiced diligently and turned up to sing in the competition. The rules stipulated that the choir consisted of a set number of voices. One of our members had not arrived, and it was almost time for us to perform.

We knew that one of the judges would be counting pairs of legs so that choirs did not have extra voices, but we didn't have our quota. I peeped out at the audience and noticed a colleague sitting on the end of a row, so I approached him quietly and brought him backstage with me.

I asked him to open his mouth in line with the fellow beside him on stage, but he wasn't required to sing. We really needed him for his legs! He thoroughly enjoyed himself. We didn't win any prizes, but it was fun.

I missed my pottery work but joined the local craft group. I attended workshops on the art of bush basket making and silk painting.

I enjoyed sewing baskets from grevillea fronds and have continued doing that for over forty years.

Having worked in the opportunity shop in Katherine, I decided to investigate such shops in Darwin, and I admit I have been op shop dressed ever since. On one visit, I bought a leaflet for five cents that gave me instructions on how to fashion earrings from folded gift-wrap paper, which I found quite intriguing.

It was the start of an on-going home business that sort of blossomed without too much effort on my part.

In the mid-90s, I gave myself a short holiday at a Japanese retreat located just behind Mullumbimby. It was owned and run by a Japanese Zen Buddhist monk and his wife. He also had a banana plantation in the hills there. There was accommodation for five guests in demountable buildings with a swimming pool and bathhouse. Fees included all the delicious meals, but we were not allowed radio or TV, and there was no telephone reception.

The countryside provided interesting walks, and our host would come over and announce that the bath was ready each evening.

The bathhouse was up an incline, open air, and we sat in lovely warm water up to our necks, gazing out through the dusk toward Byron Bay. The view was framed by bougainvillea trailing over the thatched roof.

One evening I was not feeling well, and the owner's wife came to my aid. When I returned home, I sent her three pairs of paper earrings as a little thank you gift.

Shortly after this I received a telephone call from her husband to ask if she could buy more to take with her to visit family in Japan.

This was the start of my Japanese trade which continued for the next thirty years.

Gensan acted as my agent. I sent the jewellery to him, he forwarded to Japan and arranged for payment to be made to a Swiss bank account which he also organised.

This was all to do with his business accounts, and it suited me, too, as I didn't really need the money. Later when I was doing similar offshore business in France and Italy, they also paid into this account. I have always been a champion for the education of girls, so for years I supported a girls' school in Kathmandu in Nepal from this income.

My interest in paper expanded in other directions too. I was a founding member of the Darwin Seniors' Computer Club, and I minded the club room once a week. This gave me a wonderful opportunity to follow up Iris folding with other paper folding techniques and to include all kinds of paper.

A little later I discovered Japanese paper manufactured from mulberry tree leaves and then pressed with wonderfully colourful and ornate designs. I also learnt to wrap blown eggshells to make them into decorator eggs from a kit that I sent for.

I have hardly broken an egg since then. All that I use are blown, as I need the shell as much as the egg.

By this time, I was beginning to feel that I would like to make a home for myself here in Darwin. Although my accommodation was adequate, I began to look around for something for myself and bought a two-bedroom unit in Stuart Park.

It was in a small block of six units, and I enjoyed the challenge of making my own nest as it were. I still get a laugh from the fact that I moved in with a fridge, a kitchen stool, and a queen-size waterbed. I had some crockery and cutlery and linen from my time flatting in Melbourne, and I took my time in selecting the rest of the furnishings.

Around this time, I enrolled in an aromatherapy massage course run by a local beauty salon. We were very fortunate in that the person teaching the actual massage techniques was first class and taught us very well.

I bought a portable massage table and set up my second bedroom as my massage parlour. During the course, we pupils massaged each other, and I offered massage to my friends for some extra practice.

Once I was qualified, I never had to advertise for clients; my friends and their friends became my first paying customers, and later most of my clients were referred by a psychiatrist and a psychologist.

When I queried this with the psychiatrist, he said his patients reported that one of the reasons they liked it was because I was interested enough to ask them what they had been doing to get so tense.

I had never thought about that, but I think I played 'devil's advocate' and offered way out solutions sometimes, which helped them see their problems in a different light.

Also, most of my clients were men, which might have alarmed the neighbours if they had noticed. I really enjoyed it and never had anyone ask for a little more!

Two of my clients informed me they were moving to Melbourne and wondered if I could teach them how to massage each other the way I massaged them.

We had hilarious sessions with them watching then repeating on each other. Then they both had to massage me to prove they had got the technique. They took me out to a lavish dinner as a special thank you.

I guess those sessions could have given the neighbours cause to gossip, but if they did, I never heard it.

In the mid-1980s I returned to the UK to visit, and I found that Bob was very sick. He had been diagnosed with stomach cancer and was on palliative care. Connie was in denial; everything was going to be all right, and she was very resistant to any suggestion otherwise.

There was nothing practical I could offer because they had a good network of friends round them, so I went back to Darwin with a sad heart.

A few years later, Connie died as she was preparing to move into sheltered accommodation in the village. Her brother-in-law and older sister arranged the funeral and wrote to tell me of events about a fortnight later.

I felt saddened by the fact that over all the years I had tried to please and foster a better relationship between us, but it was not to be.

When I returned to my working life, I seemed to attract the 'odd' jobs! The Territory was always short of trained nursing staff to deal with the needs of the population.

I don't know who thought up the importation plan, but I gather that enticing advertisements were placed in British nursing journals, with the result that groups of registered nurses arrived by plane into Darwin.

I was detailed to assist. I would meet the plane, collect the nurses, and take them to the hospital in a minibus. I'd show them their accommodation, then take them to buy uniforms and make sure they had

Australian currency. Some of them were destined to be sent on to Alice Springs on the Greyhound coach, so it was my duty to get them to the coach station in time and send them on their way.

I really felt for those girls! Coming from the UK they had no concept of the distance they were to travel through country that was brown, bare, and very sparsely populated. I made sure they had water, plenty of nibbles, reading matter and whatever I could think of to make the trip bearable.

I never found out if this harebrained plan worked because once they had Northern Territory registration of their qualifications, they were able to register in the other states too. That leads to what I refer to as the 'Hong Kong fiasco.'

A few years before Hong Kong was to be handed back to China, someone had the idea that there might be qualified doctors who would like to move out before the takeover.

One advertisement was placed in the *Straits Times*, a daily based in Singapore, inviting anyone interested to apply for a position in the NT.

I'm not sure what kind of response they anticipated, but there was an avalanche of applications.

A computer program was devised to access this volume, and I was given a job assisting with the data entry. Many of the applicants had similarly qualified partners that they also wished to be considered.

Several of them also indicated they would be glad if their current employer was not contacted.

When it came to selection, someone had to go to interview applicants.

In true bureaucratic style, one of the upper echelons of administrative officers was selected and he was accompanied by a trained nurse who was newly arrived in the Territory to assist in setting up the first specific mental health facility.

The in-house printer was also kept busy churning out glossy brochures detailing the joys of Territory living all in Mandarin.

These were sent over with the interview team. The result of all this labour was the arrival of a few medical men with wives and families, but it did not take them long to discover that registration with the medical board in the Territory opened the way to registration in other states.

Quite some time later I was completing a large photocopying task at the super machine reserved for important jobs.

I had gone to work especially early to be able to get access, and in just exploring the other items in that room I came across a battered box with Hong Kong labels.

My curiosity was aroused. Inside were all the glossy brochures, returned from Hong Kong. It appeared that none of the interviewees wanted any such brochures to be found in their possession. This was evidence of the fiasco that management wanted to forget.

I approached the gentleman who had led the delegation and told him that with his approval I could 'disappear' them if he thought that best.

They all went through the master shredding machine and into bags that I then sold to staff as superior garden mulch as a fundraiser for an overseas charity. I thought it was a fitting end to the saga.

A Territory mental health facility had been established, but the psychiatrist who had been behind the initiative had since died.

It was decided to get a commemorative bust made. He was known for the large black spectacles he always wore, so I was asked to go round the optical wear shops in town to find a pair of frames to be placed on the bust. When the shop assistant asked how they could help, I told them I was looking for some frames for a bust.

This pulled them up sharp and their eyes immediately dropped to my non-existent bust. I showed them the photo, and mission was accomplished. Being the odd job girl in a large organisation had quite a few lighter moments.

In 2010, I returned to the UK to visit friends and revisit Hillingdon Hospital where I completed my general nurse training fifty years previous. I had written to the current nursing administration to ask if it would be all right for me to visit and be shown around.

I also contacted two of the girls who had trained with me. On the appointed day we went back to the hospital, were given the royal tour and then entertained to lunch by the current hospital board where we each gave a general account of our lives since graduation.

Naturally, the hospital had changed considerably since our time, but we recognised plenty of spots.

By this time all my contacts in the village had died, but Margaret, the little girl who had lived opposite to me all those years ago, invited me to stay with her and her husband for a few days in the village where they now lived. She drove around all our old stamping grounds, some unrecognisable, others little changed.

The whole visit gave me much to think about and reflect upon. But my real life was in Australia, and I knew I was coming home when I landed in Oz again.

Back to work and the realities life. Since my move from Katherine Hospital in 1980, I had been 'held against' various gazetted positions, but now there was a squeeze on, and I had to be formally gazetted into an available position.

I had kept an eye out for any job within the public service or the private world, but there was nothing I really fancied.

I knew that unless I really misbehaved, they would find it hard to terminate my employment. At that time, most of the jobs within the department really needed someone with an aboriginal background. Selection by race was not allowed, but we all knew the real needs, and you didn't have to be too bright to understand the preference.

It was decided that perhaps if I did a refresher course in infant health I could be employed in that area because nurses with that qualification were few and far between.

So, down to Adelaide for six weeks. This was during winter, but I did have a few contacts to catch up with.

When I returned to Darwin, I was sent to work at the health centre in Palmerston. Their record keeping was very poor, so I completed a survey of the immunisation status of all the visiting infants and staff in between the usual duties in the baby health clinic.

After about six weeks there, I was asked to attend a meeting with the regional director to discuss my progress. When I arrived on the floor where this meeting was to take place, everyone was instantly either very busy or they had to go somewhere. I had known many of them for years, but no one wanted to be seen talking to me. I was instantly on alert.

There were three chairs in the meeting room, mine was in the corner. The regional director and the personnel manager ushered me into the room and told me that someone at the Palmerston clinic had complained about me.

I asked for details, but these were not forthcoming. Then they asked me whether I had considered early retirement! They understood that I already owned my own property, indicating, I suppose that I wasn't bothered with a mortgage. I considered this grossly impertinent and nothing to do with my employment. I terminated the meeting by saying I would discuss this matter with my union representative.

They had obviously not anticipated this move on my part, but it was the one time when I was truly thankful for my union membership.

The union representative was very sympathetic to my cause, but when she phoned to set up another meeting with her present, the regional director could not find a space in her diary for six weeks!

When she was asked what I was supposed to do during that time the Director replied that I might as well stay home and keep a low profile!

Around this time, I was also experiencing troubles on the home front. My immediate neighbour had numerous relatives and friends come to stay—often ten or more at a time if there was anything like a rock concert being held in town.

They were sleeping out in her backyard and not being very neighbourly. Any complaint on my side was taken to indicate my racist tendencies. It was a difficult situation, but salvation came from an unexpected source.

A friend introduced me to her friend who worked in real estate. We arranged for all the usual evaluations to be done, and he advertised the property very quietly, so no For Sale signs in the lawn. It was a good time to be on the market, and it sold without haggling over price within two weeks.

Now I was homeless! A friend offered me the use of a sort of granny flat under her house; no rent, but would I prune her garden instead.

I did not have very much in the way of furniture, so I put it all in storage and took great delight in posting a big SOLD sign in the lawn as I left. Then I began house hunting. The same agent took me on a viewing trip and to a mortgagee sale of relatively new but not particularly well-cared-for houses. With the cash from my previous sale and some savings, I was able to buy without taking out a mortgage, and became the proud owner of a three bedroom duplex, with a rather large garden.

Every room in the place apart from the kitchen had dreadful wallpaper, and the carpets in the bedrooms smelt of wet dog, so I had plenty to occupy my time while the department got their act together.

It also meant that I often went into my bank to enquire whether cheques had been honoured to ensure I could afford to buy another four-litre can of paint.

I repainted the whole of the inside of the house, stripped the carpets from the bedrooms and prepared it for when I could afford replacements. I was too exhausted in the evening to worry about my position, or rather non-position.

After finally meeting with administration and my union rep six weeks later, I was offered a receptionist job at the local welfare office. They claimed that was the only position they could hold me against.

They were hoping I would take umbrage and hand in my resignation, but I decided to try it out and be the best receptionist they had ever had.

It was a completely different milieu, and I quite enjoyed the challenge. They did miss me when I left, because after viewing the reports the workers presented to the magistrate's courts, I took over typing the reports for them and eliciting more detailed information from their clients when they sat in the front office with me. My approach was much less judgemental even than their case workers.

While my job as a receptionist was no challenge, it did mean that when I left the office, I didn't have to give it a thought until my next working day. This gave me time for home renovations and learning other interesting activities.

That's when I began interviewing for the Morgan Gallup Poll organisation on alternate weekends.

They provided me with interview sheets and a starting address. Once I arrived at that address, I had to turn right and keep on turning right until the entire block was complete, or I had my required interviews.

They required eight interviews each weekend. Much of the questioning concentrated on tobacco use and popular brands. I must admit to looking around for evidence of smoking, ashtrays, or table lighters, and if they did not smoke it led to a much faster completion.

The job also had its lighter moments. Arriving at a house I could hear voices inside, knocked on the door and was invited to come in. I hesitated, as people usually came to the door to see who was there, but another voice insisted that I come in please.

All the activity seemed to be centred around a bedroom, and when I arrived in the doorway it was a chaotic scene. A woman, obviously in strong labour, was on the floor surrounded by either family or neighbours. They presumed I was the midwife, hence the insistence to come in!

I assured them I was a midwife and would stay until the real one arrived. She rushed in a few minutes later; she had had a flat tyre and had to get help to change it. I left them to it, no hope of an interview there, but I did call in when I had finished for the day and was taken to see mother and baby both looking much more comfortable.

We had to bypass properties with locked gates, and if the fences were high, it was prudent to rattle the gate first to give the guard dogs time to make their presence known.

I came upon a high fence one time, so I rattled the gate; nothing stirred. I was halfway up the front path when a large Alsatian dog raced around the corner of the house with fangs bared. We both stopped in our tracks.

I calmly told the dog this was no way to greet visitors and invited him to greet me properly! I've no idea how I thought all that, but it worked. The dog came over to me in a friendly manner. The man of the house came out and was totally shocked. He had forgotten to lock the gate.

He was more than willing to give me time for an interview and to ask me just how I had charmed his dog.

I worked hard for the remuneration, but it was an interesting job, and I learnt how the other half lived. It made me very appreciative of my own living standards.

I had joined the local craft organisation several years before and regularly sold my paper earrings, decorator eggs and baskets sewn from grevillea fronds.

But, back to work. After a few months in the welfare office, I was told of my new position in the section involved the licensing of childcare centres. This was meant to be for six weeks, sort of 'on approval.' The work involved visiting centres to ensure they were operating according to the rules, to numbers of staff to children, menus provided, cleanliness, etc. I must have suited, as I stayed longer than six weeks. I quite enjoyed the change and related well to the other staff.

UNEXPECTED CHANGES

IN AUGUST 1994, I changed my GP, as I was appalled at the lack of cleanliness in the consulting rooms of his practice. I had ignored it for quite a while as the location was very convenient, and I usually only visited when I needed a script renewal. But when my GP announced that my next visit would include a pap smear, I decided enough was enough! The GP had worked in school health section all those years ago and had prescribed hormone replacement therapy at a time when I really needed that help.

On my first visit to my new GP, she enquired as to the date of my last mammogram. It had never been mentioned before, so I had never had one. I had been doing breast self-examinations, but when the GP examined me, she found a small lump. That was the start of a whole new chapter in my life.

That change of GP practice saved my life. I had been on hormone replacement therapy for several years and that fact alone should have alerted the prescribing GP to the possibility of the development of breast cancer.

I will admit that that possibility had crossed my mind, but other women were quite vocal at times about the agony of mammograms, which gave me an excuse to avoid the topic.

I found myself on what was referred to as the 'BC Roundabout.' Mammograms, visits to surgeons, the anaesthetist, the hospital, and theatre booking all in quick succession. The right mastectomy with lymphatic clearance was the first surgical operation of my life, so quite a shock to the system.

It was also the first time I had been on the other side of the blanket as it were. Jenny flew over from Perth to care for me immediately post-op, which was a great help.

The day I returned home from surgery I received a letter from the department requesting me to go into the office to discuss my redundancy. Fortunately, a friend who was well versed in public service rules fired off a reply on my behalf to the effect that this move was not allowed. They would have to wait until I was well enough to work again before that topic could be raised.

Six months of chemotherapy followed, during which I managed to contract quite severe pneumonia, so it was back to hospital and put under reverse barrier nursing for a spell. This meant that anyone coming into my room was required to mask and gown to protect me from their germs. I often heard the lunch trolley approaching but dozed off to sleep before it arrived.

When the afternoon staff arrived, I would realise how late it was. When I asked about lunch, I would be told it was long gone and too bad the lunch deliverers had not left my tray on the trolley outside my door. Wendy, another friend, visited most afternoons. She was my salvation because she brought me Heaven on a Stick, delicious ice-cream.

Two months of radiotherapy followed down in Adelaide. I was accommodated in what had been the Royal Adelaide nurses' home. Now it was being used to house out of town or state day patients and university students.

There was a mini kitchen on each floor and some of the dishes produced by the mostly Asian students were very interesting. I learnt a few tips for cooking noodles and mushrooms. I had a few nursing contacts down in Adelaide, and they kept me entertained during the weekends when I didn't have to front up for treatment.

Those who have experienced chemotherapy and radiation treatment will attest to the bone-weary tiredness it induces. I would have found it impossible to work at this time, and I was very grateful to be able to use my accrued leaves in this way. I had worked for the department for twenty-five years during which time I rarely needed to take any sick leave. There had also been times when I could not take all my leave entitlements as there was absolutely no one available to stand in for me.

This meant I had a substantial length of sick leave plus annual leave accrued, plus long service leave, so the matter of my redundancy had to be put on hold for the duration.

I finally completed all the paperwork to accept redundancy in October 1996. It was noted at the time that in fact I had 'survived' in the public service for sixteen years being held against positions but never actually gazetted into any after being my position as director of nursing at Katherine Hospital in 1976. Something of a record!

RETIREMENT AND VOLUNTEERING

❧

MEALS ON WHEELS, OP SHOPS AND MY 'ACTING' CAREER

WHILE I WAS IN HOSPITAL following the surgery, I received a visit from a member of the NT Cancer Council. She gave me information and invited me to join other women similarly afflicted at monthly meetings.

Originally, these meetings were held in their offices but when this became inconvenient, we moved our meetings to each other's homes.

Take your lunch and the hostess would provide cold drinks. It was very good therapy, as we exchanged hints and tips and commiserated or rejoiced with each other as appropriate. To this day I sometimes see a few of the original members when out shopping, and we acknowledge each other and sometimes stop for coffee.

There was a large age range amongst us, so some still had young children to care for while others were struggling to carry on working while having chemotherapy.

The original group eventually separated off into other groups, and we later added dragon boat paddling to our activities.

I finally joined the paddlers in 2006 and wished I had joined earlier. It is a very good exercise for the whole body. The camaraderie while paddling round Cullen Bay Marina was tremendous. With up to twenty women together in a boat you might have expected a few spats, or a bit of backbiting but there was none of that. We really were all in the same boat as far as our figures were concerned and we had to all pull together. The following year we went as the NT team to an international dragon boat regatta held at Caloundra in Queensland. This was my first experience of group travel and proved to be very enjoyable.

The organisers booked us into apartments and arranged buses to take us to the lakes for the events. We didn't bring home any medals, but that didn't matter at all.

The following year a group of us travelled to Sydney to take part in the dragon boat paddling in the Darling Harbour for Chinese New Year. We didn't have a full team, but we slotted into other teams that were also short on numbers. This time we booked ourselves into family rooms in small groups in a fascinating hotel in the Chinese Quarter.

I stayed at that hotel whenever I visited Sydney in later years, and when I enquired regarding its unusual layout, I found out it had originally been built as a warehouse for Chinese merchants to store their goods.

I always felt at home there, and it was very convenient both for Darling Harbour and the Convention Centre, as well as Central Station for trips elsewhere and the free bus that ran the length of George Street down to Circular Quay.

I felt I lost a lot of social contact and 'standing' when I ceased to work. Life must have a purpose of some kind, so I embarked on my varied life as a volunteer.

My first foray into this world was joining the NT Cancer Council as a volunteer. I continued as a fundraiser for the next twenty years. Together with a group of women whose lives had been touched by cancer in one way or another, we helped set up the first Daffodil Day in Darwin and continued every year after that.

Then it was The Biggest Morning Tea each year. In those days the merchandise did not arrive already assembled, so we spent hours putting kits of things together and then ferrying them to offices, shops, and clubs; in fact, anywhere we could persuade to accept them to raise funds. These kits included silk flowers on wire stems, daffodil badges, keyrings, brooches, and small teddy bears. Morning tea kits included mugs, dishes for used teabags and a handful of teabags to encourage them to invite people round for tea.

It was a lot of hard work, but we worked as a team, certainly learnt a few short cuts to get to places and became experts at 'loitering with intent' in No Parking spots while one of us dashed into the premises to deliver the goods.

We formed a committee and organised four charity lunches each year. Our mainly female lunching clientele looked forward to these events, and many of them were also our mainstays in manning stalls for any of the fundraising days held in shopping centres. We were also the base of the committee organised for the first Relay for Life held in Darwin, and most of us stuck around for the subsequent years too.

I was sorry when the lunches ceased and was quite often accosted when out shopping being asked when the next one was scheduled.

Prior to the above, I had tried my hand at helping the Red Cross with Meals on Wheels. I only did it once a week as it was quite tiring, but a great insight into the isolation of many people within suburbia. We were the only visitors many of them had during the whole day.

We tried to give them as much time as we could, but it was never long enough. We also tried to give them treats wherever possible. One man bemoaned the fact that they never served chips with the fish on Fridays, so one day we did a detour through KFC to pick up a bag of small fries for him. I was so pleased that we had done that as he died during the following week.

I volunteered at an opportunity shop all day Monday and on Friday mornings. I enjoyed my days there and worked with some other volunteers at times. Most of the pricing was left to the workers to tag 'whatever you think the client can pay.'

Not a very fair policy at all. And it proved to be my downfall. Someone else in the shop felt I should have charged a particular customer more and couldn't wait to report my sin further up the line. I was 'sacked' for being too nice! I felt that as everything in the shop was donated, our time was volunteered and we operated on the rent-free church premises, we should not be judgmental or greedy. This left me free to explore other areas.

By this time, Territory Craft had been granted the use of a small shop area in the foyer of the new Parliament House, so I volunteered to mind the shop one day per week.

It was also a good place to sell my paper earrings and grevillea frond baskets. Some days were very quiet, but we attracted a very mixed clientele with quite a number being overseas tourists. That was how I made the contacts I needed to sell my earrings in France and Italy.

I usually spent my time folding papers for more earrings while minding the shop, so if people showed interest in what I had on display I could show them the process. A French customer invited me and my stock box to join her for dinner on the evening of her visit.

Over time we developed a system whereby she mailed four sheets of gift wrap paper to me four times a year, I processed it into earrings and returned them to her in the same paper mailing tube.

She was selling them through a string of hairdressing salons in Paris. We traded like this for over twenty years, with payment being through the Swiss bank and profits going to support the girls in Nepal.

I acquired the Italian market in a similar fashion, but they would email me regarding preferred colour mixes for the coming season, and I did my best to oblige. I continued minding the shop there for nearly twenty-five years and only retired when I felt I needed more time for other pursuits.

The Museum and Art Gallery was another area for volunteering. They advertised a short course that I needed to attend prior to working there. It was sixteen weeks long; a bit daunting, but I signed up.

It was a fascinating time, and I really looked forward to Monday afternoons. We were given a very good grounding on the running of the place, talks from curators, trips behind the scenes.

We were also encouraged to increase our knowledge in any area of special interest to us, and we all prepared short talks to give to the rest of the class to practice public speaking.

Having been in the Territory for quite a while, I already knew quite a bit about Aboriginal art and crafts, so I enjoyed sharing this knowledge with visitors and groups in the ensuing years. I continued there for the next ten years.

I can't remember who approached me, but I was asked if I would be prepared to be a 'pretend patient' now and then for medical students' practical exams.

We would be given basic instructions in relation to whatever illness we were portraying, and we had to be prepared to repeat our performances multiple times depending on the number of students there were to examine.

I quite enjoyed those sessions, and it was also interesting to meet my fellow 'patients.' Some of us met socially later.

REALLY SAILING IN S.T.S ROMAN

IN 2002 I booked myself a trip on the Sail Training Ship *Leeuwin*. I travelled to Broome on a Greyhound bus to go aboard the ship. Although we were paying passengers, we were also the crew.

We sailed up the WA coast from Broome, calling in at various scenic spots on our way to Darwin. We stood watches, learnt how to raise, and lower sails, climbed the mast, steered the ship, and sat on the bow on whale watch. It was a marvellous trip.

COMPUTERS AGAIN

In 2004 the Commonwealth Government commenced a program aiming to assist the older generation to learn the intricacies of using computers. They offered packages to clubs and organisations to assist with this.

The local branch of the Council of the Aging (COTA) put up their hand. In due time, two desks, two VDUs, one printer, three chairs and a small stack of informative booklets for the students were delivered.

The concept meant that ideally two pupils could be taught at one time, with the club or organisation finding the volunteer tutors.

While I had no formal qualifications, I put my hand up together with two other members of a seniors' computer club.

It proved to be quite a difficult assignment, as often the pupils were at different stages in their understanding of keyboards and/or computer logic. I started taking one pupil at a time and found that much better.

Learning was a two-way project, too, as when I asked the pupil what they would like to explore on the internet after they had worked hard at the lesson, their requests took me to web pages I didn't even know existed. Many of them found out what a Moscow Mule was. If they couldn't think of a topic, I would ask them to find out the temperature in Moscow on that day. The mule appeared on the drop-down menu, and we just had to explore it. We all learnt it was the recipe for a vodka cocktail.

When the COTA offices were being re-organised, I began teaching people in their own homes on their own machines. This proved to be much better as the operating system on the original machines had not been upgraded enough over the years, and I had to be able to switch from the new to the old when I went to the offices.

BECOMING A MARKETEER

By about 1998 I had ceased attending church services on Sundays, and a friend asked me if I could drop in on a friend of hers who had a stall at a Sunday market.

Keith was not young, and she thought it was a bit too much for him each week. That was my introduction to market life. I enjoyed visiting him and, as he was a widower, I quite often took him some home-baked biscuits or cake for smoko during the week.

Around Christmas, he complained that he would really like to go to Sydney to visit his children and grandchildren, but he was afraid someone would take over his spot and the newspaper selling side of his business.

I volunteered to do it for him for six weeks, and I loved it. I took my paper jewellery and other crafty bits and began selling them too. When he returned, he asked me if I would like to share the stall with him, and we worked in tandem for several years.

His health was not the best, and one day he asked me to go back to the newsagents where he delivered the paper money.

When we got there, he introduced me as the new papergirl! So, I inherited the paper round and his stall space. This was a complete surprise to me, but I decided to give it a try and continued for the next sixteen years.

I must admit that there were many Sunday mornings when I would have loved to stay in my bed, especially if it was raining, but life was always full of surprises at the market. Besides, I had a duty to deliver the papers for people to read with their coffee and pancakes!

I decided that if I was going to be there, I wanted to be noticed, so I op shopped for colourful clothes. Over time, I procured a collection of different hats, all of them over-endowed with flowers.

After a while, people knew that when I put my hat on, I was ready to trade. A good friend minded her stall next door, and we would sit on the low wall opposite our wares and give the passing parade ratings for a whole range of things like 'sex appeal.'

Wearing pre-ripped jeans and shorts was the height of fashion at the time, so we often rated 'the most airconditioned clothing.'

At other times I armed myself with a clipboard and pen and approached people in the passing crowd. I told them we were doing a survey and went on to ask odd questions.

For family groups I might ask how many times a week they sat down for a meal together? This proved to be very interesting, as relatively few of them ate together even once a week.

I would then ask the parents where they had learnt their table manners and basic ethics and sent them on their way with something else to consider besides what filling they wanted in their pancakes.

Another survey asked people walking along engrossed in their mobile phones whether they had noticed the man selling brightly painted turtles round the corner that they had just walked from and other nonsensical things. My aim was to get them to enjoy the moment around them instead of playing with their favourite toy.

I had a regular clientele both for the newspapers and for my paper earrings. During the dry season, visitors to the Territory would arrive at my stall and say, 'Thank God you're still here!'

They had either visited in previous years or a friend had done so, and they had an envelope of cash and an order list of the kind or colours their friend required. Very good for trade, but it meant I had to keep producing.

The market sales combined with my overseas trading, the knitted items, crocheted bottle bags and calico dolls meant I spent most of my time restocking.

I had very little time left over to try ideas for new lines. Just after I began making the calico dolls, I was accused of being racist! When I asked for an explanation, I was told it was because I only had white dolls.

I rectified that by producing black, brown, and coffee-coloured dolls, which proved to be very popular.

One morning, a customer bought a doll for her child and mentioned they would be returning to Singapore that evening. I wished them safe travel and mentioned I would be passing through Singapore in a month's time on my way to visit family in the UK.

The next week a man I came to know as Louis arrived at my stall and bought all six dolls, I had with me. He said they were for my customer of the previous week, and he would be sending them on to Singapore.

He later contacted me via email to ask if it was possible for me to take six dolls with me as carry-on luggage for delivery to Singapore when I was passing through.

I agreed because I could always give them to friends in the UK if I didn't end up meeting his friend.

As I moved from one terminal to the other at Changi airport, I noticed a man holding a placard with 'Doll Lady?' on it.

He took me to a lounge where my original contact and her daughter were waiting. Mission completed.

Marelle then asked me to let her know when I had six more dolls ready. She would give me a date, time, and flight number to drop them off. I packed the dolls as carry-on luggage and drove slowly along the drop-off road at Darwin airport with a small doll on my dashboard.

There was always someone there to collect the parcel, and I supplied around two hundred calico dolls to Marelle this way. The money was always deposited in my overseas account.

The regular stall holders became my market family, and I was sad to give up my trading life, but it was hard work.

I considered it would be better to retire gracefully than keel over and need to have someone else pack up my gear and hope I could drive home safely. I still visit the market now and then to sit and chat with the stall holders I shared time with and have the odd pancake for old time's sake.

UNCONVENTIONAL MARKET RESEARCH, CAT WALKS AND OTHER RETIREMENT ADVENTURES

By 2015, I realised I wouldn't be able to maintain my large garden or climb up to clean the gutters of my home the next year.

A friend introduced me to her place in a retirement village, and that was the start of a whole new saga.

I visited the village again to look at available villas, put a deposit on one and began primping my house for marketing.

Until then, I had no idea of the level of stress involved in that exercise even though I only held viewings by arrangement.

It was on the market for nearly a whole year, and by November I decided to take it off the market for a couple of months to give myself a break from having to be prepared for viewings all the time.

A week after this, a prospective buyer contacted me. We were well into negotiations when she happened to mention she had viewed it once with the agent.

This rang a bell in my head relating to a sentence in the fine print of my contract with the agent, so I phoned her, intending to ask for an appointment to discuss the matter. This resulted in her launching into a positive tirade of verbal abuse, almost as though I had done it on purpose. After five minutes of this I ended the call. I then went round to see my conveyancer. He was not surprised and said she was well-known for that tactic. I went ahead and sold privately and heard no more from the agent.

RETIREMENY VILLAGE

I FINALISED THE DEAL WITH THE RETIREMENT VILLAGE and moved into what I hope will be my last home.

On my first weekend there, I was invited to my neighbour's eightieth birthday party in the community room. Many of the villagers attended as well, and I realised many of them had been friends or acquaintances during my life here in Darwin, so it was a great party.

In 2014, I joined the Darwin branch of U3A, University of the Third Age. The weekly meetings are never dull. Sometimes the topic advertised for the day may seem uninviting, but many of them are presented in ways different to our expectations, and we all benefit from having our horizons expanded. About four times a year, when there is a fifth week to the month, we hire a bus and have a day out to visit areas many of the members can't manage on their own.

Organising trips for a group of people, many of whom use walking sticks or walker frames, needs careful consideration.

Finding that I did not have to spend so much of my time replacing items sold at market gave me an opportunity to indulge myself by doing what I call unconventional market research.

Most people do much of their household shopping on automatic pilot as it were.

If you need more toilet paper, into the aisle where it's stacked, cruise along 'til you find a familiar-looking brand or the brand that's on 'special' this week and you're done!

I cruised down the aisle with notebook and pen, making notes of how the different brands attempt to persuade us to buy their product. An elderly lady stopped, looked me up and down and was obviously curious, so I told her I was doing market research! I explained a bit more, then led her to a particular stack of rolls. They claimed their toilet paper is strongest when wet! 'Just what you need,' I added.

She was not impressed and hurried off, snatching a bundle of rolls near the end of the aisle. I was still lingering in the toilet roll aisle when an old friend came by, and she related a story from her childhood. She was being taken shopping by her grandmother who asked her to remind her that they needed toilet rolls when they were in the shop. This she did as Grandma sat at the counter giving her order to the assistant. At the mention of toilet rolls her grandmother slid off the seat and took Lily to one side. 'You must never mention toilet rolls in public,' she said. Lily asked,

'Why? What are we to call them?' Grandma told her that they were "bathroom stationary." Remembering this, makes me smile every time I'm near that aisle.

I found it just as entertaining when it came to the aisle of tea products.

I remember as a child my aunt might ask for a pound of tea, please. This would be scooped from a tea chest into a paper bag, which was weighed then folded intricately. Later, tea was branded with Typhoo and Lyon brands, Earl Grey, and some green tea.

Now the tea choice has expanded exponentially with all tastes being catered for, even Lady Grey. The oddest one to me was Caravan Tea. The advertising suggested one might sense a hint of the campfires lit during its long trek across continents to your teapot. Considering that such campfires would possibly have been fuelled by burning the dung of the camels or donkeys, I'm not sure I favour it.

Now that our milk lasts longer, it has developed a life of its own. At one time there was milk from cows or goats, but now we have milk from soybeans, almonds, coconuts, and rice.

I am just waiting with bated breath for the advent of bamboo milk as it seems to be used for so much more than furniture and panda food.

Another experience not to be missed is an in-depth exploration of the pet food aisle. Some of the delicacies noted in the list of ingredients on the tins would not go amiss in a high-class restaurant.

The special treats range from especially spicy tiny biscuits to soups and tubes of puree that you may squeeze into the mouth of your overindulged pet! It isn't confined to just cats and dogs either, fish and birds also have a wide variety on offer and dogs also have the chance to munch on lambs and pigs' ears.

Watching pet owners browsing the shelves can be fascinating as they search for that special flavour or try valiantly to give their pet a diet as varied as their own. It's not just women either; some of the men are even fussier.

Others may think this a sort of mindless occupation. Perhaps it is, but I'm what may be termed 'elderly,' and I enjoy writing wry comments on these things which get printed in the U3A magazine along with reminiscences of shopping options when we were all much younger.

I see it as a reminder of all the power of advertising and to bear this information in mind when making choices.

I also enjoy writing a variety of short pieces that comment on how our habits have changed over the years.

Take such places as nail parlours and little shops offering eyebrow shaping using cotton threads. How have we managed without them until now?

The other day, I also came across a lady who still goes to her hairdresser once each week for a shampoo and set! That takes me back to the time when people went to the cinema on the same night each week and sat in the same seats.

I guess it was before we got our own TVs and access to films whenever we fancy. I do tend to feel that for all its many uses, the world wide web has a lot to answer for.

After retiring from my market stall, I still had a large variety of materials stockpiled. I gave some of it to fellow craft people who I knew would use it, but when I looked at the material ready for making more calico dolls, I decided to keep it and make it up regardless. It was especially important in 2020, the year of the COVID-19 pandemic. I knew of many families who had little or no money to spend on Christmas presents for their children, so I donated all the dolls, as well as a few other items I'd made, to each of the women's refuge houses here in Darwin. When you leave home in a hurry, you may not have time to search for the children's favourite toys.

I thought that a calico doll might help in these situations; they are soft and cuddly to curl up with in a strange bed. This has led to special requests, so I am still working in the calico doll factory and enjoying it.

I met up with Louis quite by accident a few weeks ago. He noted I was no longer running my market stall, so he was very pleased to see me and reinvigorate the doll traffic to Singapore. This time I give them to Louis, and he arranges the transport.

I can't remember when Muriel Sidebottom came into my life, but she is great fun. Many people will know of Dame Edna Everage, who is the alter ego of Barry Humphries.

Muriel Sidebottom is mine. She is an elderly lady who thinks and talks with a broad North Country accent (UK) and delights in talking about all those 'elephants in the room' that nice people never mention in public. Creating her talks usually begins in the early hours of the morning when sleep escapes me and my mind is wandering. I quite enjoy these sessions as I usually wake with a germ of an idea that develops over time until it is ready to be crafted into a talk for Muriel. Muriel sometimes even receives invitations to talk at meetings, and she is always welcome to entertain— especially the elderly in nursing home situations.

Since buying my first property in Darwin, I have also had the company of several cats. The first of these was a very aristocratic tom who walked into my place, made himself at home and behaved as though he had always lived there. Sometime later, a woman arrived on my doorstep and accused me of stealing her cat.

The cat in question came to the door, bared his fangs, and snarled at her. Enough said as far as I was concerned. He had a very grand title in line with his bearing. I named him Felix Henry Tiger Augustus! I'm sure you can imagine the hilarity in the vet's office when he went for treatments.

When we moved to my next home in Millner, I thought it was important for him to be introduced to his new neighbourhood.

I put him into his harness and lead and walked him round his garden and the street and park opposite to let him know where he belonged.

He looked forward to being taken out on the lead two or three times a day, and I became known as 'that woman who walks a cat!'

I've walked all successive cats, too, and I recommend it for getting to know your neighbourhood.

We become acquainted with the shrubbery, meet prowling bandicoots, and come eyeball to eyeball with giant grasshoppers.

The retirement village I live in now is not far from the sea, and there is a creek quite close to one boundary.

During crocodile breeding and mating seasons I am always aware of their possible presence. Along with the crocodiles, I'm never surprised when I come across a python or two either. They are non-venomous, and

I find them quite beautiful. Early morning walks are also great times to appreciate the night sky.

My time here on Earth has had its ups and downs, but life has never been dull. Hindsight is useful for helping to put things into perspective, but one cannot change what has been done. If we learn from past mistakes and move forward, life can be very rewarding.

I still look forward to whatever each new day will bring, and as you will have gathered, I'm always open for a challenge.